FIFTH GENERATION COMPUTERS

CONCEPTS, IMPLEMENTATIONS AND USES

ELLIS HORWOOD SERIES IN COMPUTERS AND THEIR APPLICATIONS

Series Editor: Brian Meek, Director of the Computer Unit, Queen Elizabeth College, University of London

FIFTH GENERATION COMPUTERS
CONCEPTS, IMPLEMENTATIONS AND USES

PETER BISHOP
Peter Bishop Associates
Richmond, Surrey

ELLIS HORWOOD LIMITED
Publishers · Chichester

Halsted Press: a division of
JOHN WILEY & SONS
New York · Chichester · Brisbane · Toronto

First published in 1986 by
ELLIS HORWOOD LIMITED
Market Cross House, Cooper Street, Chichester, West Sussex, PO19
1EB, England

*The publisher's colophon is reproduced from James Gillison's drawing of the ancient
Market Cross, Chichester.*

Distributors:

Australia and New Zealand:
Jacaranda-Wiley Ltd., Jacaranda Press,
JOHN WILEY & SONS INC.
GPO Box 859, Brisbane, Queensland 4001, Australia

Canada:
JOHN WILEY & SONS CANADA LIMITED
22 Worcester Road, Rexdale, Ontario, Canada

Europe and Africa:
JOHN WILEY & SONS LIMITED
Baffins Lane, Chichester, West Sussex, England

North and South America and the rest of the world:
Halsted Press: a division of
JOHN WILEY & SONS
605 Third Avenue, New York, NY 10158, USA

© 1986 P. Bishop/Ellis Horwood Limited

British Library Cataloguing in Publication Data
Bishop, Peter, *1949–*
Fifth generation computers: concepts, implementation and uses. —
(Ellis Horwood series in computers and their applications)
1. Electronic digital computers
I. Title
004   QA76.5

Library of Congress Card No. 85–27337

ISBN 0–85312–923–1 (Ellis Horwood Limited — Library Edn.)
ISBN 0–85312–990–8 (Ellis Horwood Limited — Student Edn.)
ISBN 0–470–20269–6 (Halsted Press)

Typeset by Ellis Horwood Limited
Printed in Great Britain by The Camelot Press, Southampton

Contents

Preface

The initiative aimed at the development of fifth generation computers
– computers with enhanced intelligence – is the most significant
advance in information technology since the invention of the transistor. It challenges every aspect of information technology: products,
markets, users and IT practitioners and, above all, the dominance of
the USA and Europe as leading IT innovators. The name, concept
and development path of the new generation all originate in Japan,
and Japan is making the running in the development stakes. Large
sums of money, and the time and energies of some of the leading
academic and industrial IT practitioners in the world are being
invested in a series of projects, some collaborative and some com-
petitive, to bring into existence a generation of computers in the
1990s based on design principles which did not even exist at the
start of the 1980s. If any national group achieves a significant lead
in the development race, that country could be the dominant force
in the IT industrial sector for a decade or more.

This book is intended to bridge the gap between the small group
of IT professionals actively engaged in fifth generation development
work and the rest of the IT community: undergraduates on computing courses and their lecturers, practitioners in all fields of computing,
managers of projects with an information technology component
and schoolteachers responsible for computing courses. It covers the

fifth generation computer initiative in breadth, and in sufficient depth to give a firm overall grasp of the subject. No prior knowledge of the background topics particular to fifth generation computers — artificial intelligence, parallel computer architectures, logic-based programming languages — is expected of the reader. A first-level knowledge of the concepts, practices and technical terms of contemporary computing is, however, assumed.

The topics covered in the book are as follows:

- A brief résumé of the development of present-day computers, drawing attention to the fundamental ideas behind information processing machines, many of which require re-examination in the light of the fifth generation programme.
- An overview, by way of introduction, of the key concepts of artificial intelligence, and a review of the progress in the field to date.
- A description of the intended overall structure of a fifth generation computer system, and outlines of the projects under way in Japan, the UK, the USA and Europe to develop fifth generation computers.
- Descriptions of the enabling hardware and software technologies which are needed to construct fifth generation computers.
- The intended applications of fifth generation computers, and some of the possible consequences of their introduction.

This book does not attempt to give a running commentary on the progress of the various fifth generation projects. It concentrates on the underlying concepts and techniques in computer architecture, software engineering, the design of user interfaces and the application of artificial intelligence which are central to the evolution of intelligent computers. Where applicable, it draws attention to the great differences between contemporary practices and what is required for the new generation. Not only will fifth generation computers make conventional computers obsolete in many fields, but they will make much computer knowledge obsolete, in particular conventional procedural programming and its associated languages, and hardware designs centred around sequential single-processor architectures.

ACKNOWLEDGEMENTS

I am grateful to a number of people for supplying reference material, some of it unpublished at the time, to assist in the research for this book: John Darlington for information about the Alice computer, Roger Bailey for material on the Hope programming language, Meir Lehman for material on software engineering and Richard Ennals for background documents about the Alvey project. All are members of the fifth generation research team at Imperial College, London. My thanks go to John Campbell of Exeter University and Brian Meek of Queen Elizabeth College for exhaustive reviews of the entire text, and helpful advice in a number of difficult areas. I am grateful for the use of the Imperial College library, where most of the research for this book was done.

4th July 1985

Peter Bishop

1

Introduction

The fifth generation represents a fundamental shift in the direction of the development of digital electronic computers. It diverges from the tradition, dating back some 35 years, of 'smaller, faster, cheaper' that has motivated the mainstream of the computing industry. The first four generations of computers are essentially variations on the original theme—an automatic data processing machine controlled by a stored program. The motivation of the fifth generation is 'more intelligent'.

However, fifth generation computers have their roots firmly in the sequence of events which has brought us to the desktop micro and the ground-hugging Cruise missile. This chapter presents a brief review of this sequence, drawing attention to those developments which are now acquiring a new significance in the light of current events. In the process it identifies a small number of fundamental concepts which are essential to an appreciation of the ideas behind fifth generation computers. It is of necessity a generalisation, a simplification, and an attribution to a few prominent individuals of concepts which evolved in discourse—particularly in the unprecedented academic, political and military collaboration which averted defeat for the Allies in the darkest days of the Second World War, and helped to bring it to a swift conclusion.

1.1 THE ORIGINS OF DIGITAL ELECTRONIC COMPUTERS

The concept of the programmable computer, as we understand it today, was first evolved by Charles Babbage (1791–1871) in his work on the design of what he called an Analytical Engine. From 1834 until his death, Babbage refined his ideas and designs for a general-purpose calculating machine, controlled by a sequence of instructions (Hyman, 1982). The machine had a processing unit, a main store, facilities for input and output of data, and the provision for step-by-step control by what we would now call a program (Babbage, 1837). The implementation of these concepts was mechanical, using complex trains of gear wheels, in accordance with the technology of the day. However, even with state-of-the-art manufacturing and quality control techniques, Babbage's designs were impossible to realise in practice. Only a few fragments of an Analytical Engine were ever built, and Babbage's ideas lay dormant for nearly a century. They formed the basis of the first (and almost the last) electromechanical computer, the Automatic Sequence Controlled Calculator (ASCC) completed in 1944 (Ashurst, 1983), and influenced the design of electronic computers.

Although no Analytical Engine was ever built, there was speculation about the limits to its capabilities, and the extent to which it could behave in a way which could be interpreted as intelligent. The most perceptive observations were made by Ada Byron, who noted that 'The Analytical Engine has no pretensions whatever to originate anything. It can do whatever we know how to order it to perform' (Menabrea, 1843).

The most intensive period in the development of digital electronic computers was the decade from 1936 to 1946. In 1936 Alan Turing published a paper in which he set out the abstract design for a computer which was not just general-purpose—it could, in theory, solve any problem which could be stated in the form of what we would now call an algorithm. In 1946 John Von Neumann and his colleagues published a document which outlined the design principles of an electronic computer controlled by a stored program. The principles sketched out in this document have formed the basis of the design of electronic computers and microprocessors to this day.

In the middle of this decade, the Second World War saw a degree of collaboration between scientists, engineers, politicians and soldiers never achieved before or since, in an effort to defeat the Axis powers by intelligence, as force alone would not prevail. In Britain the focus of this collaboration was a top-secret establishment at Bletchley Park, where a small team, led by Max Newman and including Donald

Michie and Tommy Flowers, designed a series of codebreaking computers which culminated in the electronic Colossus machines of 1943. These, based on cryptanalytic principles developed by Turing, succeeded in breaking the German High Command codes produced by Enigma machines, which were thought to be secure. It is now generally accepted that the part played by the various Bletchley machines was influential, if not decisive, in the Battle of the Atlantic, and possibly the entire war. Although details of the work at Bletchley Park remain secret to this day, several who served there have had distinguished careers in computing, including work in artificial intelligence.

After the war, the military, industrial and commercial potential of electronic computers was soon evident. The next 40 years have seen an exponential growth of computing as this potential begins to be realised. Although the rate of progress has not been steady, and there are signs from time to time of saturation of particular markets, in general this growth continues unabated. The convergence of computers, telecommunications and electronic control systems has given rise to information technology, which is likely to become the largest industry in the Western world before the turn of the century. Broadly speaking, there have been five strands of development: fundamental theory, hardware design, software design, applications and artificial intelligence. There has been continuous cross-fertilisation among the first four, but the fifth has, until recently, been somewhat remote from the mainstream. However, the isolation of artificial intelligence is coming to an end with the pressures created by the development of fifth generation computers.

1.2 THE CONCEPT OF A COMPUTER:
THE WORK OF TURING AND CHURCH

In order to understand some of the ideas of fifth generation computers, it is necessary to probe beneath the surface of the concept of a computer. Superficially, a computer is a digital electronic information processing machine, controlled by a stored program. This surface concept is the product of much deep thought, and may in the foreseeable future seem somewhat limited. The key phrase, 'information processing', was coined by Marshall MacLuhan, who was asked by IBM to explain to them, in succinct language, what computers are all about.

The key to a fuller understanding of the concept of a computer is the realisation, dating back to the turn of the century, that mathematics can be regarded as a completely abstract body of knowledge. Mathematics concerns symbols, relations between symbols, operations on symbols, and properties of these symbols, relations and operations. The fact that many of these symbols, such as those representing numbers, have a concrete realisation, does not affect their abstract mathematical properties at all. Starting with a few fundamental axioms, and precise definitions of the objects, it is possible to weave the whole complex web of modern mathematics by theorem and corollary, deduction and induction, without recourse to external reality.

In an attempt to 'round off' the development of abstract mathematics, David Hilbert posed three fundamental questions at an international congress in 1928. Firstly, is mathematics complete, in the sense that every mathematical statement can either be proved or disproved? Secondly, is mathematics consistent, in the sense that no valid steps of proof can ever lead to an incorrect conclusion? Thirdly, is mathematics decidable, in that there exists a definite method which can, in principle, be applied to any mathematical statement and which will determine whether that statement is true? Hilbert's intuition inclined him to believe that the answers to all three questions were in the affirmative, but eight years later he was proved wrong on all counts, and his concept of a 'definite method' had led to the abstract idea of a universal computer.

At the same 1928 conference, Kurt Gödel was able to show that arithmetic cannot be proved consistent within its own axiomatic system, and that it is also incomplete (Davis, 1965). Max Newman attended the conference, and lectured at Cambridge on Hilbert's questions. One of his students, Alan Turing, pondered on Newman's phrase, 'a mechanical process', and, in 1936, presented as his dissertation a remarkable paper, entitled 'On Computable Numbers, with an Application to the Entscheidungsproblem' (Turing, 1936).

Turing argued that Hilbert's third question—the *Entscheidungsproblem* — can be attacked with the aid of a machine, or at least the abstract concept of a machine. A Turing Machine (as it is now known) has the property that it can compute the value of any number which can be specified by a definite process, or what we would call an algorithm—hence the idea of computable numbers. For example, the number pi, being irrational, has an infinite decimal expansion, but its value can be stated in terms of an algorithm for its computation. Thus a Turing Machine can, given enough time, calculate the value of pi to any required precision. Although Turing presented no formal proof that a machine could have this property, he gave a number of convincing arguments, and his thesis is accepted as an axiom of the theory of computing. He used his machine concept to show that some numbers exist which are not computable by any definite method, and that Hilbert's third question therefore has a negative answer.

At the same time, almost to the day, Alonzo Church announced the same result in the USA (Church, 1936). Church used a formal notation which he termed the 'lambda calculus', to translate all the formulae of arithmetic into a standard form. Proving theorems then becomes a matter of transforming one string of symbols in lambda calculus into another, according to a set of formal rules. However, there exists no formula of the lambda calculus which can determine, in general terms, whether one string of symbols can be translated into another. Once again, the search for a 'definite method' fails in certain cases. A corollary of Church's result echoes Turing's thesis: the set of computable numbers is precisely those numbers to which there correspond formulae in the lambda calculus.

The work of Turing and Church has profound consequences for computers. First of all, a number is nothing more than a string of symbols, which may have any interpretation. An almost trivial consequence is that any number base may be used for calculations. More importantly, this is the formal reasoning behind the idea of computer data as sequences of symbols which are manipulated by the machine, but require interpretation by a user before they provide information. Most important of all, a string of symbols may be interpreted as an instruction. Secondly, a Turing Machine is universal, in that it can solve any problem which can be expressed in the form of an algorithm (in other words, it can compute any computable number). Finally, a Turing machine is, in principle, very simple. It has a single tape, which serves as input, output and memory. It is controlled by 'tables of behaviour' (programs) and can be in any one of a number of states at any time. Each operation concerns the manipulation of a single symbol on the tape, and possibly the movement of the tape by one symbol in either direction. Construction of a general-purpose computer, implementing the concept of a Turing Machine, should not, in practice, prove impossible.

Subsequent developments in the theory of computing have followed the lines set out by Turing and Church—respectively the abstract machine approach and the functional programming approach (Brady, 1977). The concept of a Turing Machine has been clarified and refined, and its properties examined in great detail. Functional programming has led to the development of such programming languages as Lisp (section 7.1), the language of most artificial intelligence work, and to the idea that a program can be regarded as a sequence of mathematical statements, and its correctness or otherwise proved by formal mathematical techniques.

1.3 THE ELECTRONIC COMPUTER:
THE WORK OF BOOLE AND SHANNON

The work of Turing and Church established the idea that a computer is essentially a symbol-manipulating machine, leaving any interpretation of the symbols to the programmer or user. The primitive operations of a computer are below the level of mathematics, and in the realms of logic. The symbols at this level are most conveniently in the form of binary digits — bits — which can represent numbers, letters, colours on a graphics display or components of a sound. The electronic switching circuits which perform these primitive operations have a close correspondence to the binary digits 0 and 1 — they can only be in one of two states.

The theoretical work which has led us to this situation can be traced back to the logic of Aristotle (384 BC to 322 BC). Aristotle set out the rules of formal logic, so that the truth or otherwise of a statement can be deduced by a definite procedure. The next major advance came with the work of George Boole (1815 to 1864), whose two works (Boole, 1848 and 1854) established that Aristotelian logic can be expressed in a formal algebraic notation. The link between logic and electronics was established by Claude Shannon (born 1916) who showed how the elementary Boolean operations can be represented by electrical switching circuits, and how combinations of circuits can represent complex logical and arithmetical operations (Shannon, 1938). Most important, Shannon showed how Boolean algebra can be used to simplify switching circuits, and that the properties of a switching circuit can be established by formal proofs.

1.4 THE STORED PROGRAM COMPUTER:
THE WORK OF VON NEUMANN

The final link in the chain of developments in the period 1936 to 1946, which led to the concept of a modern computer, was supplied by John Von Neumann (1903 to 1957) and his colleagues at USA wartime research establishments. Having worked as a consultant on the final stages of the design and construction of an early electronic

computer (the Eniac, the first and last base ten electronic computer),
Von Neumann was able to clarify the design requirements of a
general-purpose electronic computer (Von Neumann, 1945; Burks,
Goldstine and Von Neumann, 1946). The machine was to operate
on data and instructions in a binary code, stored together in memory.
A small number of registers were required, to hold such things as the
current program instruction and the current data item being processed. The machine was to operate in a repeated cycle of steps to
fetch and execute program instructions in sequence.

This description applies, to a greater or lesser extent, to all
electronic computers built since 1946. The requirement of serial
operation still holds in most individual processors, but the majority
of modern computers contain several processors working to some
extent in parallel. Increased parallelism is one of the main requirements of fifth generation computer hardware. The idea of storing
programs and data together has profound consequences. At a practical
level, it saves memory space by allowing the memory to be partitioned
flexibly between data and instructions. It means that the mechanisms for fetching data and instructions from memory are the same.
More fundamentally, it means that symbols can be treated as data
in one context and instructions in another. For example, the source
code of a high level language is instructions in the eyes of the programmer, but data as far as the compiler is concerned. The most
fundamental consequence is that programs can, in theory, modify
themselves in the light of their own operation. This seemed a very
promising line of development to Von Neumann and others in the
early 1950s, but it has not led to any major breakthroughs. At present,
self-modifying programs are frowned on, but developments in artificial intelligence may bring them back into favour.

1.5 ELECTRONIC IMPLEMENTATION:
VALVES, TRANSISTORS AND MICROCHIPS

First across the Von Neumann starting line was the Manchester
University Mark 1, a small prototype computer which came into
operation in 1948. Others soon followed, and it was only three
years later that the first commercial electronic computer (Univac)
came into service. These monster valve computers, puny in processing power by comparison with today's desktop micros, were
superseded by the end of the 1950s by transistorised versions. The
invention of the transistor, in 1948, was the event which has done
more than anything else to make computers widely accessible.

Transistors are small, cheap, and very reliable, and it soon proved possible to combine several transistors and other circuit elements in a single integrated circuit—the ubiquitous chip. The IBM 360 series of computers set the scene in the mid-1960s, and helped to consolidate IBM's dominance of the world computer market. In 1972 came the ultimate in integration—a complete processor on a single chip. By the end of the 1970s, desktop micros were commonplace, and sometime during 1982 the millionth stored program digital electronic computer was produced.

The four generations of hardware implementation—valves, transistors, integrated circuits and microprocessors, have seen an explosive growth of computing, and transition from top-secret military establishments to kitchen tables as the most popular point of use. However, most of the pioneers of the 1936 to 1946 era would be quite at home with a desktop micro, and immediately recognise its origins in the forge of the Second World War.

1.6 SOFTWARE DEVELOPMENTS

As the hardware of computers became more powerful, and at the same time more complex, it became necessary to intersperse more and more software between it and the user. It has always been the case that the detailed operation of the hardware of a computer is fully understood only by the engineers directly responsible for its design and construction. This restricted the use of early computers to just these engineers. In order to broaden the base of programmers and users, layers of software were introduced, each of which presents a simplified view of the computer to software and uers outside it.

The innermost layer, now known as the operating system, replaces the real hardware by a virtual machine, where, for example, data is transferred to and from peripheral units in logical entities (files, records, etc.) instead of physical entities. The next layer, present only during software development, is the various language translators which enable programmers to use application-oriented high level languages instead of machine-oriented low level languages. These language translators regard the instructions in a high level language as data, and transform them into an equivalent set of machine instructions, to which control is later passed by the operating system. The outermost interface, and in many ways the most important, is that presented by the applications program to the outside world. This is the user interface, which determines the interaction between the computer and the person using it. An applications program may be regarded as a way of transforming a general-purpose computer into a machine dedicated to a particular task, with the user interface as the means of interacting with this dedicated machine.

Until very recently, the user interface was regarded as a weakness in most computer systems. In many cases it was 'grafted on' to the software almost as an afterthought, without any serious consideration of the needs, knowledge or thought processes of the users. Inadequate user interfaces have been a major factor in limiting the accessibility of computers. As the psychology of the interaction between a person and a computer becomes better understood, and advances in user interface design resulting from work on artificial intelligence become better known, this situation is likely to change. The design of user interfaces (Chapter 9) is one of the key areas of fifth generation computer development.

1.7 THE SYSTEMS APPROACH

Computers are without any doubt the most complex artefacts ever produced. The fact that they are beginning to be used by a significant proportion of the population of many industrial countries, including the majority of schoolchildren, is a situation unprecedented in history. In order to manage this complexity, several conceptual techniques are required, including the ideas of layers of software and interfaces described above. The most widely used, and possibly the least widely thought about, is the idea of a system. Many computer professionals will resort to the phrase 'the system' for want of something more precise, and build up layers of confusion in the minds of their listeners.

A system is, however, a precise concept (Beishon and Peters, 1972), and one which is essential in reducing the complexity of the hardware and software of modern computers to manageable proportions. In general, a system may be regarded as a set of inter-related elements, which together achieve (or attempt to achieve) specific aims and objectives. A system may have subsystems, which comprise subsets of its elements, and which achieve subsets of its aims and objectives. In its turn, any system may be a subsystem of a larger system. A system has a precisely defined boundary, across it interacts with its environment. This corresponds closely to the idea of an interface discussed above.

Applying the concept of a system to computers simplifies matters a great deal. For example, a computer system may comprise hardware or software, or a mixture of the two. It is quite valid to describe a system in terms of its aims and objectives, or the information flows across its boundary, without specifying the components of the system at all. This leads to the idea of a module, which is a system with a very precisely defined boundary and simple interfaces, and which can be 'unplugged' and replaced by another with the same interfaces and functions, without affecting the environment of the module at all. A chip is an obvious example of a hardware module, and much effort is now concentrated on writing software which consists entirely of modules which can be unplugged and replaced in this way.

Most work on computers is implicitly carried out in terms of this systems philosophy. Computer applications, computer components and the various layers of software are described in terms of aims and objectives, boundaries and interfaces, with details of the component elements only being supplied where absolutely necessary. As the complexity of computer systems increases by at least an order of magnitude, with the advent of fifth generation computers, this systems approach will need to become more rigorous if serious misunderstandings are to be avoided.

1.8 COMPUTING IN THE EARLY 1980s

Thus we have come from the *Entscheidungsproblem* — the problem of a definite method — to the proliferation of computing in the early 1980s. The popular concepts of a computer as an information processing machine, of data as strings of symbols manipulated by a computer and interpreted by the user, and of programs which transform a general-purpose machine into one dedicated to a particular range of tasks, are the products of some of the most brilliant minds of the twentieth century. Most computer users are reasonably clear about the capabilities and limitations of computers: they can sort, select, compare and combine data, and perform calculations. They can make decisions based on the data. All this can be done at speeds which people can never emulate. But computers cannot understand the data they process. They cannot take initiatives, nor can they make sense of vague, incomplete or contradictory information. They cannot cope with information in a natural language, and although they can produce spectacular graphical displays, they cannot interpret information in a visual form. Their prowess is no more than the product of the sequences of instructions which control them and the data on which these instructions operate.

Computers have come to be the standard tools of the 'exact' sciences — physics, chemistry, and to some extent biology. They are indispensable in all branches of engineering, and the advances in aeronautics and space travel in the last forty years could not have taken place without them. But computers have not moved to the centre of the stage in such fields as sociology, economics and, above all, medicine, where the fundamental knowledge is not so precise and easily quantifiable. In these fields the highly qualified and experienced expert is the ultimate decision maker.

Much of this will change if even some of the aspirations of the fifth generation of computers are achieved.

REFERENCES

Ashurst, F. Gareth (1983), *Pioneers of Computing*, Frederick Muller.

Babbage, Charles (1837), 'On the mathematical powers of the calculating engine', in Randell (1973), pp. 19–54.

Beishon, John, and Peters, Geoffrey (1972), *Systems Behaviour*, Harper & Row, for the Open University Press.

Boole, George (1848), *The Mathematical Analysis of Logic*, Dover Publications, New York.

Boole, George (1854), *An Investigation of the Laws of Thought, on which are founded the Mathematical Theories of Logic and Probabilities*, Dover Publications, New York.

Bowden, B. V. (ed.) (1953), *Faster than Thought*, Pitman.

Brady, J. M. (1977), *The Theory of Computing Science*, Chapman & Hall.

Burks, A. W., Goldstine, H. H., and Von Neumann, John (1946), 'Preliminary discussion of the logical design of a computing instrument', in Swartlander (1976), pp. 221–259, and Randell (1973), pp. 399–414.

Church, Alonzo (1936), 'A note on the Entscheidungsproblem', *Journal of Symbolic Logic*, 1; reprinted in Davis (1965).

Davis, Martin (ed.) (1965), *The Undecidable*, Raven Press.

Goldstine, Herman H. (1972), *The Computer from Pascal to Von Neumann*, Princeton University Press.

Hyman, Anthony (1982), *Charles Babbage: Pioneer of the Computer*, Oxford University Press.

Menabrea, L. F. (1843), 'Sketch of the analytical engine', translated with additional notes by Ada Byron. *Scientific Memoirs*, 3, pp. 666–731. Notes reprinted in Bowden (1953).

Randell, Brian (ed.) (1973) *The Origins of Digital Computers: Selected Papers*, Springer-Verlag.

Shannon, Claude (1938), 'A symbolic analysis of relay and switching circuits' *AIEE Transactions* **57**, pp. 713–723; reprinted in Swartlander (1976).

Swartlander, Earl E. (ed.) (1976), *Computer Design Development: Principal Papers*, Hayden.

Turing, Alan (1936), 'On computable numbers, with an application to the Entscheidungsproblem', *Proceedings of the London Mathematical Society* 2, 42, pp. 230–265.

Von Neumann, John (1945), 'Draft report on the Edvac', in Randell (1973), pp. 383–392.

2

Artificial intelligence

We know perfectly well that, for human beings, there is a
space between totally deterministic behaviour and totally
chaotic behaviour. It is the space of intelligence. The problem
is simply that machines, in their entire history, have never
occupied that space. We may be living on the wave-front of
the most far-reaching cultural revolution in human history,
but beliefs change slowly, and we have yet to come to terms
with the fact that 'intelligence' no longer means, uniquely,
human intelligence. (Harold Cohen, computer artist, in Tate
Gallery, 1983)

Ever since Charles Babbage conceived of the idea of an automatic
computer, controlled by a sequence of instructions, the extent to
which intelligence is imparted to a computer by its human designers
and programmers has been a vexed question. Both Turing and Von
Neumann spent much of the latter parts of their careers grappling
with the problem of machine intelligence, and a small and sometimes
embattled group has kept the flame burning up to the present. The
central questions which have been attacked are:

How intelligent is a computer?

and

To what practical uses can the intelligence of a computer be
put?

These questions can be viewed from two angles. Firstly, accepting the concept of a computer as an automatic symbol manipulator which is not capable of going beyond the capabilities given to it by its hardware and software, how much intelligence can be transferred to a machine under these conditions? To what extent is human intelligence capable of expression in terms of symbol manipulation? The second approach is to re-examine the fundamental concept of a computer which has come to us from the work of Babbage, Turing, Von Neumann and others, to see whether any of the implied limitations can be relaxed or removed. Most of the research into artificial intelligence to date has concentrated on the first approach; much fifth generation work is in the second category.

Underlying these questions is a more fundamental difficulty: the notion of human intelligence is not clearly enough defined to provide a firm basis for concepts of artificial intelligence. For this and other reasons, there is no universally accepted definition of the term 'artificial intelligence' (Boden, 1977) and the two broad lines of research — into fundamental theories which underlie large classes of applications, and into heuristic methods which apply to specific situations — have sometimes been at odds. Years of intensive research have produced tantalising glimpses of the way ahead, but very little substantial progress. For example, although computers are now quite capable of playing grandmaster level chess, the problem of identifying the chess pieces jumbled up in a box and placing them in their correct positions on a chess board is quite beyond even the most sophisticated computer-controlled robot.

In Britain, research into artificial intelligence suffered a severe setback with the publication of the Lighthill Report (Lighthill, 1972), which concluded that most artificial intelligence applications have so much variety that computers will be caught in a 'combinatorial explosion' in dealing with them. This is to say that in the small number of situations (such as chess-playing) where artificial intelligence has made some progress, the number of possible combinations of events, although very large, is just manageable using carefully designed rules and strategies. However, in nearly every real-life situation, the number of possibilities is too large to consider individually. For example, computers can quite easily be programmed to distinguishing between simple shapes such as cubes and pyramids, but distinguishing between more complex shapes, such as different types of nuts and bolts, or people's faces, is almost impossible. Much of the work in artificial intelligence is concentrated on developing search strategies to reduce the number of possibilites in any particular situation, but this did not carry sufficient weight to reduce the impact of the Lighthill Report. The emergence of fifth generation computers, which are based on developments in artificial intelligence, has begun to reverse the decline in artificial intelligence research in Britain, but the number of experienced practitioners in the field remains very small.

This chapter examines some notions of human intelligence, and presents a working definition of the concept of artificial intelligence. It investigates ways of representing knowledge on a computer and reviews the various fields in which artificial intelligence research is making progress.

2.1 NOTIONS OF INTELLIGENCE

It is generally accepted that some people are more intelligent than others, and that most people are more intelligent than chimpanzees, and that most chimpanzees are more intelligent than tapeworms. Furthermore, most people would concede that even tapeworms do possess some minimal level of intelligence. In a similar way, most people would agree that a word processor is a more intelligent machine than a typewriter. Although a rough relative scale of intelligence can be established in this way, the defining qualities of intelligence remain elusive. Intelligence is related to the ability to recognise patterns, draw reasoned conclusions, analyse complex systems into simple elements and resolve contradictions; yet it is more than all of these. It contains an indefinable 'spark' which enables new insights to be gained, new theories to be formulated and new knowledge to be established.

Intelligence can be placed in a hierarchy of which the lowest level is information. Information consists of the facts (or purported facts) which form the raw material for the higher levels. Information is easily acquired — it can be written down, entered into a computer system, or learned by rote. The next level is in the area of knowledge: associations between facts, mathematical formulae, etc. Knowledge is not as easily acquired as information — it requires a complex and poorly understood process of learning. Next comes intelligence which operates on information and knowledge. The capability for intelligence is innate, and is realised to a greater or lesser extent through knowledge and experience. At the top of the hierarchy is wisdom, which frequently has mystical or religious overtones, and which is even more difficult to define than intelligence.

This heirarchy can also be examined from the point of view of language. Information can easily be represented as words, numbers or some other symbols. Knowledge is generally expressed in linguistic or mathematical form, and the representation of knowledge is one of the greatest challenges for the developers of fifth generation com-computers. Intelligence is astride the upper limit of language: instances of patterns or deductive reasoning can be written down, and certain general principles enunciated, but the creative 'spark' of intelligence is beyond expression in language. Wisdom is almost entirely beyond the reach of language: attempts to trespass in words at this level are generally confirmed to riddles of the 'What is the sound of one hand clapping?' variety.

A further problem arises in the use of language to describe aspects of intelligence, either natural or artificial. This is that the terms used in the descriptions are 'loaded' with various philosophical, psychological and even political assumptions (Boden, 1977). The word 'intelligence' itself is a good example. To some, of a behaviourist persuasion, the term has a fairly narrow and precise meaning, and is capable of a certain amount of measurement. To others, more humanistically inclined, the term carries a great depth of meaning. The problem of the use of words with no agreed, precise definition is never-ending — words are defined in terms of other words, and used with motives which are open to debate, etc.

It is becoming increasingly clear from studies in psychology that what we understand as the conscious, rational mind is only the tip of the intelligence iceberg. Beneath are layers of subconsciousness, which operate in ways which are only dimly understood and which only occasionally present coherent images to the surface of consciousness. Nevertheless these layers of the subconscious are an integral part of the whole mental process, a feature often ignored in work on artificial intelligence. One of the most intelligent people who has lived this century, the artist Salvador Dali, has made it clear that the vision which underlies his work is the imagery presented to him by his subconscious mind.

The physiology of the brain and nervous system is, in more ways than one, a grey area. We are beginning to understand how signals are carried along nerve cells, and, principally through crude studies of accident victims, learning which areas of the brain are responsible for which mental processes. We know that the 'processing' carried out within the brain is a very highly parallel operation, and that there is no clear distinction, in 'hardware' terms, between 'processing' and 'memory'. We know that different types of cells are found in different parts of the brain, but that some parts can, under certain circumstances, take over the functions of other parts. In other words, the brain is fault-tolerant to a considerable extent. However, we have little idea of what constitutes the basic mechanisms of thought and memory, and seem a long way from finding out. From time to time analogies are drawn between the performance of computer circuits and that of the brain. Quantitative comparisons are sometimes drawn between processing powers, operational speeds or memory capacities of computers and the human brain. None of these stand up to close scrutiny — they are comparing digital information processing in silicon semiconductor materials with a biological process which is orders of magnitude more complex, and about which we know very little.

From a philosophical point of view, the theory of knowledge has gone through a number of changes over the last few centuries, until the position has been reached where the prevailing view is that nothing is known with absolute certainty:

> The way in which knowledge progresses, and especially our scientific knowledge, is by unjustified (and unjustifiable) anticipations, by guesses, by tentative solutions to our problems, by conjectures. These conjectures are controlled by criticism; that is, by attempted refutations, which include severely critical tests. They may survive these tests; but they can never be positively justified: they can neither be established as certainly true nor even as 'probable' (in the sense of the probability calculus). (Popper, 1963)

Any systems which automate knowledge are subject to this limitation.

The conclusion which one must draw from these various lines of reasoning is that there is no firm baseline of 'natural' intelligence against which to measure artificial intelligence, and that developments in artificial intelligence have taken place on theoretical foundations which are still the subject of intense debate. These have been some of the most serious problems in the development of artificial intelligence. They have been circumvented in a number of ingenious ways, as examined in the next section.

2.2 MACHINE INTELLIGENCE

The very first computers were soon labelled with the phrase 'electronic brain' (Hodges, 1983), and the extent to which they were capable of intelligent behaviour immediately became a topic of major concern. There were various attempts to draw close parallels between the computer and the nervous system, for example in the later work of Von Neumann (Von Neumann, 1951), and of the neurologist, W. Ross Ashby (Ashby, 1952). These led to intense discussion and speculation, but very little substantial progress.

In 1950, Turing approached the problem of machine intelligence rather as he had approached the general concept of a computing machine in 1936. Having attended a discussion on 'The mind and the computing machine' at Manchester University in 1949, he produced a paper (Turing, 1950), which set out his own ideas on the subject. This paper contains what is now fairly widely accepted as a practical test for artificial intelligence: If there are two identical terminals in a room, the one connected to a computer, and the other operated remotely, in some way, by a person, and if someone using the two terminals in unable to decide which is connected to the computer, and which is operated by the person, then the computer can be credited with intelligence.

Turing's test circumvents all the problems with the philosophical, psychological and physiological notions of intelligence mentioned in the previous section. It regards intelligence itself as undefined, but intelligent behaviour as recognisable. It has been criticised from a number of angles (it is completely subjective, it gives no indication how an intelligent computer system might be designed, it compares things which are not even in the same dimension of measurement, etc.), but it has a wide measure of support. It leads to one of the least controversial definitions of artificial intelligence: 'Artificial intelligence is the science of making machines do things that would require intelligence if done by people' (Minsky, 1968). One benefit of this definition is that it allows for levels of intelligence, and measures the degree of intelligence against the task being performed. A computer calculating a weekly wage is exhibiting a certain measure of intelligence, as would a computer if it were to deduce the fundamental process of cancer growth. It is this incremental advance in the frontier of machine intelligence which underlies the concept of fifth generation computers.

No computer system has come anywhere near to passing the Turing test in general terms. Nevertheless, it would take a very good chess player in the 1980s to be able to tell whether he or she were playing against a computer or a human opponent. Most car drivers are unaware which parts of their cars have been assembled by robots, and which by manual workers. The progress in these and other aspects of artificial intelligence is described in the remaining sections of this chapter.

2.3 INFORMATION AND KNOWLEDGE

Conventional data processing is based on information; artificial intelligence is based on knowledge. As discussed in the previous section, the processing of knowledge requires strategies which keep the number of possibilities to be considered in any particular situation to a manageable level. A central problem for artificial intelligence, therefore, is an adequate representation of knowledge on a computer. On the one hand, the representation must be 'rich' enough to be of practical use. On the other hand, it must be simple enough to form the basis of automatic strategies which will draw valid and useful conclusions from the knowledge, within the hardware and software limitations of the host computer.

The general line of approach which has been most successful is to represent a knowledge-based system in terms of three levels (Alty and Coombs, 1984). At the lowest level are associations between objects. For example, using an English notation, 'high temperature is a symptom of influenza', or, more formally:

symptom-of (high-temperature, influenza).

Associations of this form are known as sentences or propositions in knowledge-based systems. The relations themselves (such as 'symptom-of') are known as predicates. The objects within a proposition may be constants (for example 'high temperature', 'influenza'), or variables, for convenience denoted by lower case letters as in:

symptom-of (x, y)

which means that x is a symptom of y.

Propositions may relate more than two objects, or be an assertion about a single object. For example:

symptom-of (distended-stomach, malnutrition, infant)

meaning that a distended stomach is a symptom of malnutrition in infants, and:

disease (influenza)

meaning that influenza is a disease.

Propositions may include a probability or weighting factor, using some convenient scale. For example:

symptom-of (high-temperature, influenza, 8)

means that a high temperature is a symptom of influenza with a weighting factor of 8, on a scale of (say) −10 to 10, where negative weights mean a probability of a reverse correlation. Use of weighting factors enables reasoning to take place using 'fuzzy' logic, and contradictions between conflicting evidence to be resolved.

The second level of representation of knowledge is sets of rules which connect propositions. To quote a grossly over-simplified example:

If symptom-of (x, y) and displays (z, x) then suffers-from (z, y)

which means that if x is a symptom of disease y, and patient z displays symptom x, then patient z suffers from disease y.

The above is a specific instance of the general construction:

If A and B then C

where A, B and C are propositions. Constructions of this nature may be manipulated by a set of general rules of inference, such as:

If A implies B, and B is false, then A is false.

These general rules may be used to generate new propositions or rules from an existing bank of propositions and rules connecting them, or to test the correctness of propositions or rules in the light of given propositions and rules. The rules of inference, and the formal procedures for applying them are known as predicate calculus.

The problem, in any particular situation, it to know in what sequence to apply the rules of inference to the given set of propositions and rules, without setting off a combinatorial explosion. For example, if it is established that:

A implies B

then any additional proposition may be included in such constructions as:

A and C implies B,

A and D implies B,

etc. This gives rise to the third level of representation of knowledge on a computer: a strategy to control the application of the rules of inference to the particular rules pertaining to the situation. Development of effective strategies has been one of the most difficult problems facing researchers in artificial intelligence.

There have been two broad lines of approach to this problem. One has been to attack the problem in general terms, and to try to develop consistent strategies for drawing inferences from sets of rules. This work has stayed within the confines of formal logic, and has led, amongst other things, to the development of the Prolog programming language. The other line of approach has been to develop specific inference techniques which are applicable in certain areas. This latter approach has been in the mainstream of artificial intelligence work, and has led to the development of expert systems. Both of these lines of development are taken up again in later sections of this book, and both are essential to fifth generation computers. At present there are a number of systems of logic, each with its own set of axioms and theorems, and each applicable to a class of problems in artificial intelligence (Turner, 1984).

A serious difficulty which underlies all the approaches to knowledge representation by computer has been pointed out by Edward De Bono (De Bono, 1969 and 1985). All the techniques of knowledge representation at present under development attempt to fit the knowledge into fixed structures within a computer. This static representation contrasts with the dynamic processes of human intelligence, where the patterns and associations of knowledge are constantly changing, especially during a learning process. In De Bono's words: 'A truly thinking computer will have to be a self-organising system, and that's quite a different concept from our normal concept of information systems'.

2.4 GAME-PLAYING PROGRAMS

Game-playing is one area in which computers have achieved more than was originally thought possible. Twenty years ago few people would have taken the idea of a chess-playing computer seriously; today large computers are approaching grandmaster level, while home microcomputers can play a more than adequate game. At the time of writing, the world backgammon champion is a computer system. The success of game-playing software is due to a fairly clear understanding of some of the strategies commonly used in playing games, and to the large memories and fast processors of modern computers — in other words a combination of brute force and intelligence.

As an example of the brute force approach, the game of noughts and crosses has only a few hundred possible configurations. A computer playing the game can quickly follow every consequence of each possibility for its next move, right through to the end of the game, and thus select the most favourable move. In the game of chess, this cannot be done, even on the most powerful computers in existence, since the number of possible moves multiplies so rapidly. The most successful chess programs achieve the right balance between the breadth of the search (the number of possible moves investigated), the depth of the search (the number of consequent moves investigated for each possibility) and the measures of favourability applied when evaluating the moves.

An example of a consistent strategy which has been used in game-playing programs is the minimax rule. Each possible move is evaluated in terms of the potential benefits to the opponent, assuming that the opponent makes what is to him or her the most advantageous counter-move. The move which minimises the benefit to the opponent, assuming the opponent takes maximum advantage of the move, is the one chosen, hence the name minimax. Although the minimax rule requires, in theory, a search to the end of the game from each possible move, a number of techniques have been developed to 'prune' the search tree once it is established that a particular move is inferior to an alternative already considered (Boden, 1977). An arbitrary limit is set to the 'depth' of the search, depending on the power of the computer playing the game. In many games it has been proved that the minimax strategy is far too conservative, and more adventurous strategies are used.

2.5 REASONING PROGRAMS

Game-playing programs are a specific case of a more general class of reasoning programs. These have been used to solve the kind of pattern-recognition problems found in IQ tests, and to solve problems in formal logic. The capabilities and limitations of programs of this sort are well demonstrated by the use of computers to assist in the proof of the celebrated Four Colour Theorem (Appel and Haken, 1976). It has been known for centuries that no more than four colours are needed to colour in any map, so that no two adjacent zones have the same colours. This theorem was finally proved with the aid of a computer program in 1976.

The proof is in two stages. Firstly, the program generates approximately 1800 basic map elements, and shows that all maps are made up of topological combinations of these elements. Then the program considers each map element in turn, and shows that, in every case, no more than four colours are needed to shade the areas so that no adjacent ones have the same colours. Although many mathematicians have objected to the inelegance of the proof — it requires such a large number of separate subproofs — and some reject it outright, no better method has been found, and the computer-assisted technique remains the definitive proof. This method of proof, where a problem is broken down into a large number of subproblems, may be applicable to other situations, particularly proving the correctness or otherwise of computer programs.

2.6 NATURAL LANGUAGE RECOGNITION

One of the conclusions reached in Chapter 1 is that computers cannot, in general terms, interpret continuous passages in a natural language. Nevertheless, computers can cope with individual words and phrases, and extended passages of natural language in specific topics. One of the main thrusts of fifth generation computer development is to improve the ability of computers to respond to natural languages, to the extent that large numbers of voice-driven applications become feasible.

Much of the work on natural language recognition by computer derives from the work of the linguist Noam Chomsky (for example, Chomsky, 1965 and 1968). Chomsky has shown that languages can be classed in different levels, in order of their underlying complexity. At the highest level (the context-sensitive grammars) are the natural languages, and at the next level below them (the context-free grammars) are programming languages. Chomsky also showed that there is a 'deep structure' underlying statements in natural languages, and that equivalent statements in different natural languages have the same deep structure.

When one considers the problems people have in dealing with natural languages, it is quite easy to see the enormous difficulties raised by trying to transfer a linguistic capability to a machine. The first obstacle is one of syntax. Natural languages are composed of structures such as sentences, which are constructed according to formal rules. For example, the sentence:

The cat sat on the mat

can by analysed (or parsed) as:

<subject> <verb> <object>

where <subject> ('the cat') can be further parsed as

<article> <noun>

etc. The problem with parsing is that the rules for sentence construction are very complex, there are many exceptions, and the rules are gradually modified as languages evolve.

However, in order to understand a passage, syntax analysis is not enough. The semantics or meaning of the piece depends on the context and what has been said before, as well as the meanings of individual words. Very often an alternative interpretation of a single word can alter the meaning of a whole passage. As an example, consider the following two syntactically identical sentences:

Dogs must be carried

and

Hard hats must be worn.

Few people would even notice that their meanings are completely different, let alone have any trouble interpreting them. However, without contextual information, a computer could not distinguish between the possible interpretations.

An example of the progress which has been made in natural language recognition is the system developed by Terry Winograd named Shrdlu (Winograd, 1972). Shrdlu has an environment consisting of a flat surface (the 'table'), a box, and a number of blocks of varying shapes (cuboids or pyramids), sizes and colours. There is an imaginary robot arm, which is able to pick up a block and move it to another position. Interaction with the user is via a graphics display of the current state of the blocks, and by messages exchanged with the robot arm in English. The robot can respond to instructions, and answer questions about the state of the blocks, or its own past actions. Because the system has a large bank of contextual information about the state of the blocks, and the rules which govern their behaviour (e.g. pyramids can be stacked on blocks, but not vice versa), and it keeps a record of all previous interactions with the user, it is able to interpret most potentially ambiguous instructions. For example:

User: Pick up a red block.
Shrdlu: OK. (Graphics display shows red block being lifted.)

User: Put in the box.

Shrdlu: By 'it' I assume you mean the block I am holding. OK.
  (Graphics display shows block being put in the box. If the
  box already contained a pyramid, this would first be removed.)

User: Pick up the pyramid.

Shrdlu: I don't understand which pyramid you mean. (No action
  takes place, since the user has not previously referred to a
  pyramid.)

Winograd's system, comprises three programs working together
with a fairly complex interaction. The first is a parsing system which
interprets and constructs the syntax of the statements exchanged
with the user. The second is a semantic system which infers the
meanings of the verbal exchanges. The third is a deductive system
which applies the instructions to the blocks, and determines the
responses of the robot arm. The semantic system requires information from both the syntax system and the deductive system in
order to work out the meaning of each statement.

Shrdlu illustrates the strength and the weakness of natural
language interpretation by computer. On the one hand, it can respond
to a very wide range of requests, and can cope with words such as
'this', 'that' or 'it' in sentences. On the other hand, it is limited to
its closed world of coloured blocks. In order to cope with this very
small world, it is a very large and complex program. It does, however,
indicate the kind of approach — syntactic and semantic analysis with
reference to an underlying knowledge base — which is required when
designing natural language processing systems.

2.7 IMAGE RECOGNITION

Babies born with certain sight defects must have them corrected very
soon, otherwise, even if their eyes are put right later, their brains will
never be able to interpret the visual signals. This is a somewhat dramatic reminder that the faculty of vision is only partly to do with
our eyes, and to a much greater extent to do with the way the brain
processes the visual information reaching it. It is no coincidence that
the word 'see' is often used with the meaning of 'understand'.

Although computers can construct graphics displays of breath-
taking complexity, far less progress has been made with the converse
problem of interpreting visual information, supplied, for example,
by a video camera. The ground rules of visual interpretation are

Euclidean geometry and topology (the theory of connected surfaces, etc.), but these are far less helpful as a theoretical basis for computer vision than might be expected. Euclidean geometry gives a precise account of how to construct a two-dimensional representation of a three-dimensional scene, but the problem of computer vision is essentially the opposite — how to re-create a three-dimensional scene, and recognise objects in it, from a two-dimensional picture. As Edward De Bono puts it: 'Pattern recognition in the brain is extremely simple; because of the way the brain is wired up, it can't help recognising patterns. Whereas pattern recognition in computers is extremely difficult, because the approach is totally opposite. The architecture of the brain is very different from the architecture of computers' (De Bono, 1985).

The artificial intelligence approach to this problem has been to construct sets of 'rules of thumb' for the interpretation of particular visual patterns, and to apply these to various specific situations. Most systems start by identifying the boundaries of the various objects (a much more difficult task than it first apears), and then deducting their shape and other properties. Programs have been developed which will decide correctly, in the majority of cases, whether the silhouette of a person is that of a man or a woman, and identify the kinds of blocks which are used in the Shrdlu system described above. A special-purpose hardware system known as Wisard has been developed at Brunel University, which will recognise the identity of an individual, by matching a video picture of the person's face against a bank of stored images. It is now becoming clear that the key to intelligent image processing is a very high degree of parallel processing, perhaps to the extent of having a microprocessor for every pixel in the graphics display (Duff, 1982).

2.8 EXPERT SYSTEMS

The most successful area of development under the umbrella of artificial intelligence has undoubtedly been expert systems. An expert system is a computer program which matches a competent level of human expertise in a particular field. Expert systems are a product of the line of research which has avoided seeking general solutions to the underlying problems of intelligence, and concentrated on transferring specific aspects of human intelligence to computers. Expert systems are one of the main application areas of fifth generation computers, and are discussed further in section 10.6.

2.9 PROGRAMMING LANGUAGES FOR ARTIFICIAL INTELLIGENCE

As discussed at the end of Chapter 1, there have been two broad approaches to the development of the concept of a computer. The one is the abstract machine approach, and the other is the functional programming approach. The latter approach has become closely involved with the development of programming languages for artificial intelligence research. Several of these languages are likely to have a major influence on fifth generation computer programming languages, and they are included in the discussion in Chapter 7.

2.10 CONCLUSION

In spite of difficulties with fundamental concepts, and disagreements between practitioners, significant progress has been made in the abstruse and sometimes controversial field of artificial intelligence. In particular, the ability to transfer a measure of intelligence from person to computer in specific fields has been demonstrated. One of the biggest challenges, in the view of several leading practitioners, is the automation of human common sense. The rate of progress in artificial intelligence is likely to accelerate dramatically in the next few years, as the work assumes its place as a central part of the theoretical basis of fifth generation computers.

REFERENCES

Alty, J. L., and Coombs, M. J. (1984), *Expert Systems: Concepts and Examples*, National Computing Centre.

Appel, K., and Haken, W. (1976), 'Every planar map is four colourable', *Bulletin of the American Mathematical Society*, **82**, 5, 711–712.

Ashby, W. Ross (1952), *Design for a Brain*, Chapman & Hall.

Boden, Margaret A. (1977), *Artificial Intelligence and Natural Man*, Harvester Press.

De Bono, Edward (1969), *The Mechanism of Mind*, Penguin Books.

De Bono, Edward (1985), 'Starteck: thinking about self-organising systems', in *Computing: The Magazine*, 25th April 1985.

Chomsky, Noam (1965), *Aspects of the Theory of Syntax*, MIT Press.

Chomsky, Noam (1968), *Language and Mind*, Harcourt, Brace & World.

Duff, M. J. B. (1982), 'Parallel architecture and vision', in SPL International (1982).

Hodges, Andrew (1983), *Alan Turing: The Enigma of Intelligence*, Unwin.

Hofstadter, D., and Dennett, D. C. (eds.) (1981), *The Mind's I*, Harvester Press.

Lighthill, James (1972), *Artificial Intelligence: Report to SERC*, HMSO.

Minsky, M. L. (ed.) (1968), *Semantic Information Processing*, MIT Press.

Popper, Karl (1963), *Conjectures and Refutations: The Growth of Scientific Knowledge*', Routledge & Kegan Paul.

SPL International (1982), *The Fifth Generation — Dawn of the Second Computer Age*'.

Tate Gallery (1983), *Harold Cohen*, Tate Gallery Publications.

Turing, Alan (1950), 'Computing machinery and intelligence', in *Mind*, October 1950; reprinted in Hofstadter (1981).

Turner, Raymond (1984), *Logics for Artificial Intelligence*, Ellis Horwood.

Von Neumann, John (1951), 'The general and logical theory of automata', in *Von Neumann, Collected Works*, Vol. V, Pergamon Press, 1963.

Winograd, Terry (1972), *Understanding Natural Language*, Academic Press.

3

The fifth generation programmes

The idea of a fifth generation computer was first given wide publicity at an international conference in Tokyo in October 1981 (Moto-Oka, 1982). Both the term 'fifth generation computer' and the revolutionary designs implied by the term were of Japanese origin – the product of two years of advanced research at the Japan Information Processing Development Centre (JIPDEC). The impact on those attending the conference – prominent figures from the computing industries of most Western countries – was similar to that of the launch of the Soviet Sputnik in 1957. It was immediately realised that fifth generation computers represent a radical break with tradition in computing, and that if their ambitious designs are even only partly realised, they will make most conventional computers obsolete. The industrial, economic and political significance of these possibilities was not lost on any of the participants, nor on the commercial organisations and countries they represented.

The idea of a international collaborative effort to develop the notion of a fifth generation computer into marketable products was raised at the time of the conference, but this was later rejected in favour of independent research and development efforts on a regional or national basis. By 1984 there were five major programmes under way: the Japanese Icot programme, the MCC and Darpa projects in the USA, the Esprit initiative in the EEC and the Alvey programme in Britain. Relations between the groups are a mixture of collaboration and competition: there is a free flow of theoretical information through published papers and international conferences (for example, SPL International, 1982 and 1983, and Scarrott, 1983), but most of the projects have severe restrictions on the dissemination of specific details of products under development.

3.1 JAPAN: THE ICOT PROGRAMME

If the project succeeds, it will be for us, like killing three birds with one stone. First, it will meet the needs for new-type computers that will grow with the increasing sophistication of information utilisation. Second, it will contribute toward the growth of the electronics industry that will form the core of the Japanese industrial structure in future. Third, it will help to internationalise Japan to a great extent. (Osamu Seki, Director, Electronics Policy Division, MITI, quoted from Kikuchi, 1983).

The most ambitious, and the most highly centralised, of the fifth generation development projects is the Japanese. The Japanese initiative is coordinated by the Institute for New Generation Computer Technology (Icot), set up in April 1982 under director Kazuhiro Fuchi, with an $855 million budget for a ten-year, three-phase programme (Fuchi, 1983). The project is regarded as a critical element in Japan's industrial performance, and continuing prosperity, in the 1990s and beyond. Seven broad areas of research have been identified (Fig. 3.1), covering the main design requirements of fifth generation computers. Each broad area is subdivided into more specific topics for development, with provision for transfers of intermediate results at a number of stages. One of the priorities is to incorporate software advances into hardware design: an intelligent computer-aided design (CAD) system for VLSI chips is an important aspect of the project.

The first of the three phases is one of feasibility studies and designing the tools to be used for future research. Researchers have been equipped with Personal Sequential Inference (PSI) desktop computers to undertake preliminary studies. Initially there is an emphasis on Prolog programming language for software investigations, and a move towards dataflow architectures as a hardware model. The second phase, commencing in 1985, is one of testing the two basic mechanisms of fifth generation computers: knowledge bases and inference processors. The final phase, commencing in 1989, is the construction of a prototype fifth generation computer.

Basic application systems
    1.1   Machine translation system
    1.2   Question answering system
    1.3   Applied speech understanding system
    1.4   Applied picture and image understanding system
    1.5   Applied problem solving system

Basic software systems
    2.1   Knowledge base management system
    2.2   Problem solving and inference system
    2.3   Intelligent interface system

New advanced architecture
    3.1   Logic programming machine
    3.2   Functional machine
    3.3   Relational algebra machine
    3.4   Abstract data type support machine
    3.5   Data flow machine
    3.6   Innovative Von Neumann machine

Distributed function architecture
    4.1   Distributed function architecture
    4.2   Network architecture
    4.3   Database machine
    4.4   High-speed numerical computation machine
    4.5   High level man–machine communication system

VLSI technology
    5.1   VLSI architecture
    5.2   Intelligent VLSI CAD system

Systematisation technology
    6.1   Intelligent programming system
    6.2   Knowledge base design system
    6.3   Systematisation technology for computer architecture
    6.4   Database and distributed database system

Development supporting technology
    7.1   Development support system

Figure 3.1 The Icot fifth generation computer development programme.

As is customary in Japan, there is close collaboration between the researchers at the Icot centre, most of whom are on secondment from IT corporations, and the computing and telecommunications industry. The basic research and first-level development is carried out within Icot; the specific product development is contracted to (Japanese) electronics and computer corporations. The Icot programme is under the umbrella of the Ministry of International Trade and Industry (MITI), which has been the coordinating group behind Japan's rapid postwar economic growth.

The Icot project is regarded in the West as a major advance from Japan's traditional role as a perfecter and mass producer of established technology. Some doubts have been expressed at the ability of researchers brought up in an environment of fixed, short-term goals to achieve the level of innovation required. The specific performance targets set by the Japanese teams for various elements of a fifth generation computer are also the subject of some scepticism in the West. However, if the Icot programme is even only partially successful, it will place Japan firmly in the front rank of information technology innovators for many years to come.

3.2 THE USA: DARPA AND THE MCC

Response to the Japanese fifth generation initiative in the USA has been constrained by traditional and legal restrictions on business practice. The idea of a national collaborative venture for advanced research has only one precedent: the Nasa programme to put the first man on the moon. Collusion between rival corporations in advanced computer development could violate the anti-trust laws which are a cornerstone of American capitalism. An exception is any activity with potential defence applications. For this reason, much of the USA fifth generation research and development is being coordinated by the Defense Advanced Research Project Agency (Darpa), with a $50 million 1984 budget, and a potential call on up to $1 billion. Darpa is a funding and specification agency, which channels the requirements of the defence establishment into contracts with commercial corporations for implementation. Projects consistent with the concept of a fifth generation computer sponsored by Darpa include voice recognition and speech synthesis, natural language analysis, relational databases, image processing and advanced semiconductor design.

The other USA fifth generation initiative is a commercial venture, the Microelectronic and Computer Technology Corporation (MCC), founded by William Norris of Control Data Corporation, and with an annual budget in excess of $50 million (Gannon, 1983). The MCC is a consortium of IT corporations, each of which pays a minimum $100 000 entry fee in return for access to research results and proto-type designs. Membership includes Digital Equipment Corporation, National Cash Register and chip manufacturers Motorola and National Semiconductor. The objective of the MCC is to carry out applied research and pre-competitive product development on aspects of fifth generation computers. Emphasis is being placed on computer-aided design techniques for VLSI chip production, image processing and expert systems. Directing the project is Robert Inman, whose background includes the US Navy and the CIA. IBM is not a member of the MCC, but is no doubt spending some of its $2 billion annual research and development budget on fifth generation work.

One aspect of fifth generation computer development where the USA has an established lead is basic research in artificial intelligence. With the decline of interest in and funding for this work in the UK in the 1970s, a significant number of leading academics moved to the USA, strengthening the teams already established at several leading American universities. The traditionally strong ties between academia and industry in the USA mean that advanced work is quickly made available to corporate developers of fifth generation systems.

3.3 THE EEC: ESPRIT

At the 1982 Versailles summit conference, EEC leaders, acting on a suggestion by President Mitterand, agreed to investigate the possibility of a collaborative programme of advanced information technology research and development. The outcome was the European Strategic Research Programme in Information Technology (Esprit), planned by an informal group of leading European IT companies meeting with EEC Information Technology Commissioner Vicomte Etienne Davignon. Its £450 million budget took more than a year to be formally approved by all the layers of EEC bureaucracy, but a number of projects were subsequently started. The ten-year pro-gramme is intended to cover a broader range of projects than the Japanese initiative. In addition to the artificial intelligence aspects, such topics as office automation are included. The Esprit programme is likely to merge into the wider Eureka initiative which aims to coordinate research and development in a number of high-technology fields.

The Esprit programme has a small executive which evaluates research and development proposals submitted by IT companies and academic institutions with the Community, and preferably by international consortia of such organisations. Approved projects are given up to 50% EEC funding on the condition that the results of the work are exploited within the Community. Typical of the projects is a scheme to investigate the design of software development environments for logic programs, carried out by a team at Imperial College, London. Several of the other project grants have gone to the UK semiconductor manufacturer, Plessey, for work on VLSI chips and computer-aided design and manufacture (CAD/CAM) research.

The Esprit project has been accused of excessive political and bureaucratic meddling, and of discrimination against small firms in its funding policies. There is also the endemic uncertainty over funds, given the precarious state of EEC finances. However, it is generally accepted that a Europe-wide initiative in the field of Fifth Generation computers is essential in order for companies and academic institutions in the region to maintain their presence in the world IT community.

3.4 THE UK: THE ALVEY PROGRAMME

> The issue before us is stark. We can either seek to be at the leading edge of these technologies; or we can aim to rely on imported technology; or we opt out of the race. The latter we do not regard as a valid option. (Report of the Alvey Committee, 1982)

The British response to the Japanese fifth generation initiative was to appoint a committee to investigate the matter and publish a report. Chaired by British Telecom Technology Director, John Alvey, the committee included leading IT industrialists and academics, and heard evidence from all sectors of the United Kingdom IT community. Its report, published in October 1982, recommended a five-year national programme for Advanced Information Technology, with a budget of £350 million. It proposed a decentralised 'collaborative effort between industry, the academic sector and other research organisations, with Government backing' (Alvey Report, paragraph 8.1). The plan was accepted almost without reservation by the British Government in April 1983, with an allocation of £200 million state funds, the balance to be provided by industrial participants in the programme.

A small executive was set up, under director Brian Oakley, assisted by seven sector directors on secondment from the computing industry. Their brief was to set overall objectives for the areas of development covered by the programme, and allocate state funds for up to 50% of the cost of approved projects. The first projects included demonstrator systems to test the feasibility of fifth generation ideas in practice.

The Alvey Report identified four key enabling technologies required to bring Fifth Generation computers into existence: software engineering, VLSI chips, intelligent user interfaces and intelligent knowledge-based systems (IKBS). These four lines of development are reflected in the overall structure of the Alvey Directorate. Alvey funds have been allocated only to projects undertaken by UK companies or consortia, and all research findings must be developed into products within Britain. There is a measure of collaboration between the Alvey and Esprit projects, to ensure that there is no duplication of effort between the two programmes.

There are several research and development projects under way in the UK which, although initially not funded by the Alvey programme, are relevant to fifth generation computers. These include a prototype dataflow computer which has been under development at Manchester University since 1976, and an abstract data type machine due for completion at Imperial College in 1985 for use in advanced program language design (section 5.6). (Both of these projects have subsequently secured Alvey funding.) Donald Michie, Colossus team member and artificial intelligence pioneer, has co-founded Machine Intelligence Research Affiliates (Mira), a consortium of seven IT corporations, including ICL and several oil companies, to develop IT products which utilise artificial intelligence concepts and techniques. In London, Imperial Software Technology (IST) has been formed in collaboration with Imperial College to make software engineering skills available to the IT industry. The Inmos Transputer (section 5.7) and its associated Occam programming language (section 7.4), scheduled for availability during 1986, are designed with fifth generation applications in mind.

The Alvey programme was criticised for not establishing a centre of excellence on the Icot model, and for its low ceiling of state funding, which effectively excluded small companies from participating. However, it is clear that the wide consultation undertaken in the preparation of the Alvey Report gave rise to a programme which was in accordance with the realities of the state of information technology in Britain, and gave a sense of direction and purpose to the industry which was desperately needed. The importance of projects with potential social benefits was stressed, and the dangers of abusing the power of advanced information technology was widely debated. There are signs that the collaboration between IT companies and academic researchers, which is an essential prerequisite for progress in a programme as complex as the fifth generation computer project, has begun to bear fruit. In retrospect the Alvey project may be regarded as an effort to create a certain momentum of advanced information technology research and development in Britain, so that subsequent stages, undertaken without state subsidies, would have a firm base from which to work. It is expected that many of the collaborative partnerships established during the Alvey programme, particularly between industrial and academic organisations, will be continued.

3.5 CONCLUSION

The fifth generation idea, having captured the imagination of the IT community at the beginning of the 1980s, now has a somewhat lower profile as the teams in the participating countries confront the enormous obstacles facing them. Other countries such as Canada have launched smaller-scale projects in the same overall direction, and there are indications that the Soviet Union has embarked on an equivalent programme. The importance attached to the programmes varies somewhat from one country to another: the Japanese project is regarded as central to the country's continued economic and social prosperity. In Britain the work is being undertaken amid increasing disquiet that the country's balance of trade in information technology is steadily worsening, and the possibility of the country losing its place in the IT 'first division' altogether. Similar considerations apply throughout the rest of Western Europe. The British and European programmes are ultimately subject to political control, and have finite allocations of funds and timespans of existence. In the USA the fifth generation programme is part of the ongoing effort by the IT corporations to maintain their leading positions. The MCC has the advantage of being a permanent institution, able to draw on state subsidies when they are available, but essentially free from official control.

None of the practitioners is under any illusions about the difficulty of the task, and the fact that it may not succeed. Nevertheless, the step-by-step approach adopted in all the programmes means that intermediate developments can be absorbed into the mainstream of information technology as soon as they become available. If any of the national groups develops a significant lead on the others as the fifth generation projects progress, that country or region will have the chance of becoming the dominant IT power for a decade or more.

REFERENCES

Alvey, John (1982), *A Programme for Advanced Information Technology*, HMSO.

Fuchi, K. (1983), 'The direction the FGCS project will take', *New Generation Computing* 1, 1, 3–9.

Gannon, T. F. (1983), 'Background paper on the Microelectronics and Computer Technology Corporation (MCC)', in SPL International (1983).

Kikuchi, Ahira (ed.) (1983), 'Discussion at the start of the fifth generation computer systems project', *Icot Journal* No. 1.

Moto-Oka, T. (1982), *Fifth Generation Computer Systems: Proceedings of the International Conference on Fifth Generation Computer Systems, Tokyo, Japan, October 19–22 1981,* North Holland.

Scarrott, G. C. (ed.) (1983), *The Fifth Generation Computer Project: State of the Art Report,* Pergamon Infotech.

SPL International (1982), *The Fifth Generation – Dawn of the Second Computer Age.*

SPL International (1983), *Fifth Generation World Conference, 1983.*

4

Fifth generation computers — overall structure

The epitome of contemporary computing – the supercomputer – consists of banks of high-speed processors, operating in parallel on arrays of numbers or closely coupled in a pipeline, with further processors to pass the information to and from secondary storage. The total assembly achieves a very high throughput of data, and makes use of densely packed VLSI chips. The processing power of these supercomputers continues to grow exponentially, their physical volume and power requirements decrease with each new model, and their prices reduce in real terms. However, they bear no resemblance at all to fifth generation computers, nor are they likely to be compatible with them. Furthermore, their vast information processing capabilities will seem insignificant by comparison – if the designs set out in this chapter are realised even only in part.

In broad terms, a fifth generation computer is conceived as a 'series of interconnected database and parallel processing machines, accessed by means of an intelligent inference machine which can [amongst other things] accept problem statements in a natural language' (Bramer, 1984). Its main function is not information processing, in the conventional sense, but drawing inferences from knowledge bases. It is to incorporate a much higher degree of intelligence than contemporary computers, approaching that of a human expert in certain circumstances. The main application area of fifth generation computers is expected to be the solution of highly complex problems, ones which require a considerable measure of reasoning, intelligence and expertise when carried out by people. This requires that all that is known at present about artificial intelligence — and a lot more besides — is incorporated into the design of fifth generation computers. The target date for the first full implementation of these concepts is the early 1990s.

In spite of their awesome capabilities, fifth generation computers are meant to be used by people who are not necessarily computer specialists. To make this possible, one of the main lines of development of fifth generation computers is intelligent user interfaces — interfaces which enable communication between person and computer to take place in a way which is simple and natural to the user. These are in some contrast to contemporary user interfaces, which are more attuned to the requirements of the computer than to the knowledge, inclinations or familiar way of thinking of the person using it. Interactions in a natural language, or a large subset of one, and interfacing by means of sound and pictures, are central requirements of intelligent user interfaces.

The fields of application which fifth generation computers are intended to tackle include medicine, geological prospecting, social administration, management, of both human and physical resources, research in the humanities, and a variety of tasks which require language processing and translation. They are all characterised by large bodies of knowledge, much of it empirical or heuristic, complex underlying principles which are often incompletely understood, and little assistance from contemporary computer systems. They are also all areas of major social significance, both to industrial nations and to developing countries which, by the 1990s, may have a sounder technological infrastructure than they do at present, and thus be in a position to derive great benefits from these developments.

4.1 THE OVERALL STRUCTURE OF A FIFTH GENERATION COMPUTER

The proposed structure of a Fifth Generation computer was announced at the conference in Tokyo in October, 1981, which marked the launch of the Japanese program. It was the outcome of two years of study and research at the Japan Information Processing Development Centre (JIPDEC, 1981). Almost its only point of similarity with existing systems is its basis on VLSI architecture. In every other way, both hardware and software, it represents a radical departure from conventional computing. Although many practitioners have expressed reservations about the Japanese model, it provides a useful starting point for the discussion, and has, in its overall concept if not in every detail, been accepted as the basis for further development by the teams in the various countries.

Fig. 4.1 shows what has become known as the 'basic configuration image' of a fifth generation computer. In practice, each implementation will be 'structured according to function' from the elements shown in this diagram. It is also envisaged that machines of the type shown here will be connected in local or wide-area networks, each of which will provide additional levels of distributed processing.

Fig. 4.1 is a systems diagram; it attempts to show operational relationships between a number of hardware and software elements. Looked at 'horizontally', it has a hardware layer, a software layer, and an external interface to applications systems, as might be expected. Looked at 'vertically', it becomes clear that each aspect of the functionality of a fifth generation computer — problem solving and inference, knowledge base management and intelligent interfacing — requires its own hardware and software support mechanisms. These mechanisms interact at various levels, but are essentially autonomous. The extent and nature of the parallelism this implies is far beyond anything at present in operation or under development for conventional computers.

At the risk of over-simplifying the situation, the three 'vertical' elements of Fig. 4.1 are shown in Fig. 4.2. This shows the conceptual structure of a fifth generation computer, without attempting to portray the supporting mechanisms involved. The three aspects of the system — knowledge bases, inference processing and intelligent interfaces — are discussed below.

The basic processing operation of a fifth generation computer is not numerical computation, but drawing logical inferences. Accordingly, the performance requirements are expressed in logical inferences per second (lips). The target for the problem solving and inference mechanism of a fifth generation computer is in the range 50 to 1000 million lips. By comparison, contemporary computers operate at between 10 000 and 100 000 lips. The storage capacities of the memory units which support the various processors are likely to be three or four orders of magnitude greater than the largest computer memories at present in operation: the knowledge base management systems are targeted for capacities of up to 1000 gigabytes (JIPDEC, 1981), as against 100 megabytes for a present-day supercomputer.

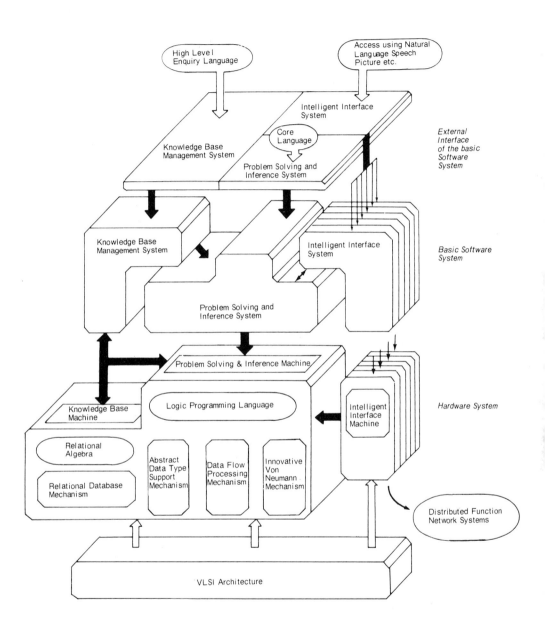

Fig. 4.1 – The basic configuration image of a fifth generation computer. (Reproduced by permission of Japan Information Processing Development Center.)

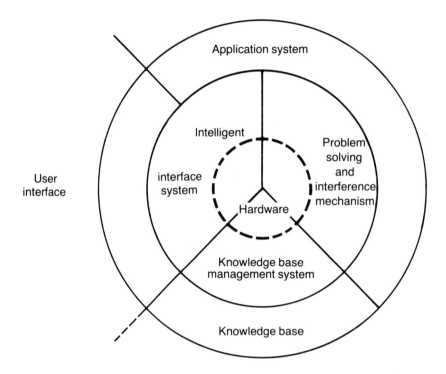

Fig. 4.2 — The elements of a fifth generation computer.

4.2 KNOWLEDGE BASE

The element of a fifth generation computer in some sense 'furthest' from the user is the knowledge base. This is envisaged as a very large store of knowledge, which may be structured as associations between objects, rules for the formation of new associations and strategies for applying the rules, as described in section 2.3. The essential feature of a knowledge base is that it must be able to support the processing of vague, incomplete and possibly contradictory information.

A knowledge base is likely to be an extrapolation of current developments in relational databases, where data is stored in tables, with each row in a table being an instance of a relationship between the categories of object. A simple example of such a database is one with two tables, one relating names to addresses, and the other relating names to telephone numbers:

Table 1			Table 2	
Name	Address		Name	Telephone number
J Brown	12 Elm Street	Ely	P Adams	01 345 6789
A Smith	23 High Street	Crewe	J Brown	0353 65437
M Young	The Drive	Fritton	M Young	049379 3421

A fundamental operation of relational databases is the ability to join tables by common elements, to produce additional relations. In the above example, the two tables could be joined by Name, producing a combined table (containing only two rows) of Name, Address and Telephone number. Note that the operation is not applied to individual data elements, but to two entire tables, which in practice may contain millions of elements, and it results in the creation of a third table.

The theory behind data manipulation of this sort is known as relational algebra. Fifth generation computers are likely to require both software and hardware mechanisms to carry out relational processing. The software for relational database processing is now fairly commonplace, but the hardware which can manipulate data, not as individual elements, but as complete tables in a single processing step, is a matter for research and development. In order to achieve the overall performance requirements of fifth generation computers, such dedicated hardware, shown in Fig. 4.1 as a 'relational database mechanism', will be essential.

A vital conceptual tool for the handling of large quantities of complex data is the notion of an abstract data type. For example, the relations embodied in the tables above may be considered in abstract, without regard to their implementation as a structure of rows and columns. At a high level, a program controls the processing of these abstract objects, leaving lower levels of hardware and software to deal with their particular implementation and storage in memory or on backing store. The notion of abstract data type enables the intrinsic logical properties of data objects to be defined, and the objects to be manipulated in terms of these properties. It brings about great simplifications in programming, and allows the logical and the physical aspects of a programming system to remain separate. As applied to databases, the notion of abstract data types gives rise to the concept of data independence, whereby the logical structure of a database is entirely independent of its representation on any particular physical medium.

On contemporary computers the various levels of data abstraction are dealt with principally by layers of software, but this is unlikely to be sufficient for the fifth generation. At a fairly low level, a transformation mechanism is required, implemented in hardware, to map the logical properties of abstract data types onto their physical representations. This is shown in Fig. 4.1 as an 'abstract data type support mechanism', and it is a key element in knowledge base processing as well as inference processing.

4.3 INFERENCE PROCESSOR

The 'central' element of a fifth generation computer is an inference processing mechanism. This interacts with the intelligent interface system to communicate with the user, and with the knowledge base mechanism to draw on the knowledge resources, while addressing itself to the fundamental task of solving the kinds of problems which will fall within the orbit of fifth generation computers. As in the case of knowledge base processing, dedicated hardware and software are required.

The basic task of inference processing is drawing conclusions from evidence, as discussed in section 2.3. These may be 'definite', as the example of that section:

> If symptom-of (x, y) and displays (z, x) then suffers-from (z, y)

or may include an element of uncertainty:

> If symptom-of (x, y, probability > 0.7) and displays (z, x, probability > 0.9) then suffers-from (z, y, probability $= 0.6$)

The software for inference processing is likely to be based on developments in the area of logic programming, at present exemplified by the programming language, Prolog. A program in Prolog contains declarations of relationships existing between various elements, and rules allowing conclusions to be drawn from relationships. The first of the above inference constructions is in the form of a statement in Prolog. The essential difference between Prolog and other declarative languages, and conventional procedural languages such as Pascal, is that the logical assertions in a Prolog program are all valid simultaneously. They are not meant to be applied sequentially, and many of the problems associated with logic programming stem from the limitations of current sequential processors. Implicit in inference processing and the logic programming software which supports it, is a very high degree of parallel processing. Prolog and other potential fifth generation computer languages are discussed in Chapter 7, and intelligent knowledge-based systems are the subject of Chapter 8.

In order to achieve the inference processing throughput figures mentioned earlier, a dedicated logic processing hardware mechanism is required for fifth generation computers. This is referred to in Fig. 4.1 as a 'problem solving and inference machine'. It requires direct hardware support for logical assertions of the type discussed above, based on a mechanism which can cope with the vast size and complexity of a 'real' inference problem. These problems are likely to require millions of inferential assertions, many of which are to be interpreted in parallel.

A promising hardware architecture for this situation is known as dataflow architecture, in which a large number of discrete (sequential) processors are connected in a network. Each processor 'triggers' its operation as soon as it has received a complete set of data on which to operate, and it passes its results down the network as soon as the operation is complete. In this way the data flows through the network, which is structured to reflect the extent of parallelism inherent in the particular application. See sections 5.4 and 5.5 for further details.

Finally, and much more speculatively, the JIPDEC model includes an 'innovative Von Neumann mechanism' at the base of its problem solving and inference machine. As outlined in section 1.4, the essential features of a Von Neumann processor are symbolic coding of data and instructions, no fundamental distinction between data and instructions, and sequential processing of instructions via a small number of processing registers. All computers constructed to date are variations on this theme, and it is quite possible to implement a dataflow network using conventional Von Neumann processors. However, there is scope for a wide range of innovation around this basic concept, and the very high level of parallelism required of all aspects of fifth generation processing may require something substantially different. See section 5.9.

4.4 INTELLIGENT USER INTERFACE   *you dont wk Er 8*

The catchphrase 'user-friendly' has managed to attract, satisfy or delude users of the first four generations of computers, but it is far too shallow a concept for the fifth generation. What is friendly to an aerodynamics engineer in a research establishment will not do for a paramedical worker in Ethiopia. For the fifth generation the tables must be turned: the computer must come to terms with the nature and way of thinking of its user, and not vice versa. The interaction between person and computer needs to be a natural extension of the human approach to the task: 'When compared with conventional systems, man—machine interface will be closer to the human system' (JIPDEC, 1981). Although the user may be an expert in a field such as medicine or geology, only an elementary level of computer literacy can be assumed.

There will possibly still be a place for character-based interaction between user and computer, using conventional keyboards and display screens, but this is likely to be limited to the application areas where it is most appropriate, such as entering or updating the knowledge bases used in more dynamic situations. The current tendency for mouse and icon control of programs may well be developed into fifth generation applications. However, two main channels of communication between fifth generation computers and their users are almost certain to be natural language and visual displays. As discussed in sections 2.7 and 2.8, progress in both of these areas has been hampered by fundamental problems in the past.

In the case of natural language, the operational goal is to automate a large enough subset of a language to be useful in particular situations. To return to the above example, a paramedical worker in Ethiopia uses a limited subset of a medical vocabulary, in which the terms have a fairly precise meaning, and the overall context of the interactions is known to the computer. In a similar way, image processing will be used in reasonably well-defined circumstances, such as industrial assembly plants, surgical operations (probes into organs returning fibre-optics images) and satellite repairs in space. In each case the class of objects to be recognised is sufficiently limited to come into the range of current research and development work. See Chapter 9 for details.

More generally, the psychology of the interaction between a person and a computer is coming under intensive study in order to provide a firm basis for the design of intelligent user interfaces. Whichever technique is chosen for a particular application, it will require a dedicated software and hardware system to support it, interacting with the inference processing systems of the computer at a variety of levels.

4.5 FIFTH GENERATION HARDWARE AND SOFTWARE

A few general points about the hardware and software of fifth generation computers are in order at this stage. All the indications are that, in spite of the conceptual break with previous computer generations, the hardware of fifth generation computers will be based on very large scale integration of semiconductor components. The scale of integration will be at least two orders of magnitude above the current state of the art: hundreds of thousands of discrete elements per chip. Whether silicon remains the basic ingredient, or is replaced by another semiconductor such as gallium arsenide, is a matter for research and development. See Chapter 5 for details.

Most contemporary data processing programs are of the order of tens or hundreds of thousands of lines of source code in a procedural language such as Cobol or Ada. It is certain that each of the layers of software in a fifth generation computer will require millions of lines of source code, in logic-based languages such as Prolog or dataflow languages such as Occam. Furthermore, since the hardware of each type of fifth generation computer will be much more closely tailored to its application area than is the case at present, it will be impossible in most cases to develop the software on the ultimate host machine. This and the size and complexity of the programs means that advanced techniques of software engineering, using custom-built software development environments, are required in order to bring fifth generation software packages into being. These may include facilities to prove the correctness of program modules by formal techniques, as if they were mathematical theorems. The software engineering aspect of fifth generation computers is discussed in Chapter 6.

4.6 CONCLUSION

Computers are already the most complex artefacts ever devised, but the projections for fifth generation computers are set to raise the level of this complexity by several orders of magnitude. The challenge facing the development teams in the participating countries is to manage this complexity, and bring into existence, in a very tight timescale, an aggregation of functional elements each of which lies at or beyond the frontiers of current research. At the end of the road lies the goal stated in the original report (JIPDEC, 1981): 'intelligence will be greatly improved to approach that of a human being'.

REFERENCES

Bramer, Max (1984), *The Fifth Generation: An Annotated Bibliography*, Addison-Wesley.

JIPDEC (1981), 'Preliminary report on study and research on fifth-generation computers', Japan Information Processing Development Centre, in Moto-Oka (1982), pp. 3—89.

Moto-Oka, T. (ed.) (1982), *Fifth Generation Computer Systems: Proceedings of the International Conference on Fifth Generation Computer Systems, Tokyo, Japan, October 19—22 1981',* North Holland.

5

Fifth generation hardware

The most spectacular developments in computing in recent years have been in hardware. Since the first microprocessor in 1972, the number of functional elements per chip has steadily increased. Single-chip memories have moved rapidly through 8K, 16K, 64K and now 256K capacities, with megabyte memory chips already at prototype stage. The price per unit of performance or storage has steadily decreased, and reliability of these complex solid-state devices is extremely high. However, these recent developments seem insignificant by comparison with what is required for fifth generation hardware.

The main thrust of hardware developments to date has been to implement conventional processor and memory architectures more and more compactly in silicon. This has led to a widening 'semantic gap' between the high level requirements of a computer — as a problem-solving machine working in a language such as Pascal, Prolog or Ada — and its low-level architecture. One of the motivations of fifth generation hardware development is to narrow the semantic gap: to develop 'effective support functions to be implemented at the computer architecture level in realising knowledge information processing systems' (Aiso, 1982). Therefore, in addition to being substantially more powerful, fifth generation hardware will be based on radically different architectural concepts from those in vogue today.

One line of approach is to consider the hardware and software aspects of the design of the new computer systems as a whole, and allow the 'mutual interaction of algorithm, architecture and technology to establish a balanced design satisfying the system goals' (Allen, 1982). This view needs to be taken in conjunction with the requirements of the overall architecture of a fifth generation system as an interacting assembly containing a knowledge base processor, an inference processor and an intelligent user interface. The balanced designs which satisfy the performance goals of the three subsystems may not turn out to be very similar. However, there is a strong feeling that there must be a single underlying architectural concept for fifth generation computers, and possibly a common 'kernel' language (roughly equivalent to the machine language of contemporary systems) (Treleaven, 1982).

5.1 VERY LARGE SCALE INTEGRATION

Although the architecture of fifth generation computers is fundamentally different from what is in use today, and the storage and processing requirements are orders of magnitude higher, the fundamental hardware technology remains the same — very large scale integration of semiconductor components. Gallium arsenide is being investigated as an alternative to silicon, and novel ways of cooling very large, densely packed chips are being tried out; but what is required appears to be an extrapolation of the trends in operation at the moment — packing more and more components into the same small area of silicon.

The complexity of state-of-the-art VLSI chips is vividly illustrated by an analogy drawn by Charles Seitz. If the first integrated circuits were as complex as the street grid in a small district, 'the ultimate one-quarter micron technology will likely be capable of producing chips with the intricacy of an urban grid covering the entire North American continent' (Seitz, 1980). The constant reduction in size of chip elements gives rise to enormous engineering and quality control problems at every stage of chip fabrication. At present the constraint is the width of a conducting path on a chip — currently of the order of half a micron, but likely to reduce to a quarter of a micron during the timescale of the fifth generation computer programme. The precision of the chip fabrication stages has to increase continually to cope with these requirements, and some measure of redundancy has to be incorporated into chip designs to compensate for the inevitable flaws. The ultimate limiting factor is the speed of light: the speed with which electrical signals propagate along a conductor. In order to achieve nanosecond performance, all the processing elements of a computer have to be contained within a volume of a 30 cm cube (light travels approximately 30 cm in one nanosecond).

One VLSI technique with a somewhat chequered history is wafer-scale integration. The conventional chip fabrication process is to form a few hundred identical chips on a circular slice − a wafer − of silicon crystal. A seemingly obvious step forward is to use the whole silicon wafer for a single chip, some 5 cm square. This approach was tried unsuccessfully by Gene Amdahl's Trilogy Corporation in the early 1980s. The problem is one of quality control: conventional chips are tested before they are separated from their wafer, and defective ones discarded. In practice the yield varies considerably, but is seldom over 90%. In order to be usable, a chip made by wafer-scale integration must be perfect, or close enough to perfection for the redundancy in its design to cope. With a potential for several millions of functional elements, and a complexity an order of magnitude above the largest conventional chips, the required standard of manufacture has not yet proved possible in practice.

Assuming that the fabrication aspects of VLSI are dealt with, the major problem is chip architecture: how to manage the multiplicity and complexity made possible in arrays of millions of functional elements. Many of the latest approaches (section 5.8) are aimed at gaining the most from large combinations of simple elements, with short and regular control paths (Mead and Conway, 1980). The novelty is the nature of the processing elements and the degree of parallelism incorporated into the arrays.

5.2 PARALLEL PROCESSING

It is agreed by all concerned that the key to fifth generation computer architectures is a much higher degree of parallelism than is incorporated into computers at present. It is likely that there will be a number of layers of parallelism: closely coupled processing elements reflecting the parallelism inherent in inference or knowledge base processing operations, looser coupling between the various subsystems in a fifth generation computer, and distributed processing across local and wide area networks of computers.

At present there are two types of close-coupled parallelism implemented in computers: processing arrays and pipelines. Processing arrays are vectors of identical processing elements which act synchronously to perform identical operations on arrays of data.

Pipelines are used for multi-stage operations such as floating-point multiplication, where each element of the pipeline carries out one step of the operation, and passes its intermediate result to the next element. Operations on successive sets of data can take place at intervals of one step. Parallel processing of this type, known as 'regular' parallelism (Gurd, 1982), will undoubtedly find a place in fifth generation computers, but mechanisms to deal with irregular parallelism are the main topic for research. Three approaches are worth further discussion: parallel control flow, dataflow and graph reduction.

5.3 PARALLEL CONTROL FLOW

Traditionally, each step of a program is executed in sequence, under the control of a single program counter which determines the low-level operation to be carried out next. The flow of control is implicit in the structure of the program. For example, the control module of a Pascal-type program for payroll processing might be as follows:

```
begin
     read (salary_record);
     calculate_gross_wage (salary_record);
     calculate_income_tax (salary_record);
     calculate_national_insurance (salary_record);
     calculate_net_wage (salary_record);
     write (salary_record)
end
```

Each statement in the module is a call to a more detailed processing procedure. It turns out that (under the present UK tax regime!) the calculation of income tax and national insurance are independent of each other. Therefore, if a parallel computer system and programming language were available, the control module could be written as follows:

```
begin
     read (salary_record);
     calculate_gross_wage (salary_record);
     parallel
          calculate_income_tax (salary_record);
          calculate_national_insurance (salary_record)
     end;
```

        calculate_net_wage (salary_record);
        write (salary_record)
    end

The tax and national insurance processing procedures are called at
the same time. They execute in parallel, and the control module
waits until both are complete before continuing. Programming
languages such as concurrent Pascal and Ada (section 7.3) have
facilities for operations of this sort, but it remains to be seen whether
this approach, which is only a slight variation on conventional
sequential processing, will be adequate for the radical demands of
fifth generation architectures.

5.4 DATAFLOW ARCHITECTURE

For a number of reasons, one of the most promising architectural
models, certainly for the inference processing subsystem of a fifth
generation computer, is dataflow architecture. It can cope with
irregular as well as regular close-coupled parallelism, it is flexible
and extensible, it has the potential for very high data throughputs,
and it reflects, at hardware level, the type of parallelism inherent in
inference processing (Tanaka, 1982). The Japanese fifth generation
programme is strongly committed to a dataflow approach, and it is
becoming increasingly prominent in UK projects.
    To introduce some of the concepts of dataflow architecture by
way of example, consider again the Prolog-type statement:

        If symptom-of (x, y) and displays (z, x) then suffers-from
        (z, y).

Assuming that a contemporary computer were able to evaluate one
predicate or one binary boolean operation in one processing step,
a sequential compiler might translate the example as shown below,
using the intermediate boolean variables A and B:

        A = symptom-of (x, y)
        B = displays (z, x)
        suffers-from (z, y) = A and B.

The three resulting low-level language instructions would be carried
out one after the other on a conventional computer. However,
another way of representing the structure of this statement is in the

form of a graph, as shown in Fig. 5.1. (An equivalent version of this graph structure would have been produced by the compiler as an intermediate stage before obtaining the three low-level language instructions above.) A dataflow interpretation of this structure is to use three processing elements as shown in Fig. 5.2, two of which operate in parallel.

This simple example illustrates the central idea of dataflow architecture: a network of processing elements is set up, which reflects the logical structure of the task to be carried out, and items of data flow between the elements. Each element operates at its own pace, and waits until it has a complete set of intermediate inputs before it 'fires'. There are two techniques for the control of such a network. In the totally data-driven approach, each element waits passively for data to arrive, whereas in the demand-driven regime each element issues requests 'upstream' for data when it is ready for it (Sharp, 1985).

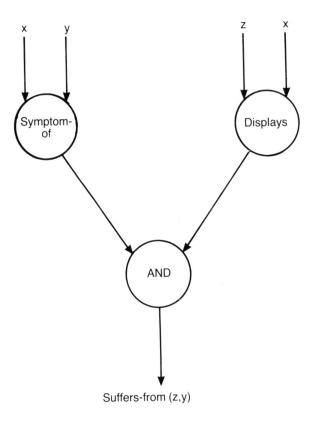

Fig. 5.1 – Graph of multiple inferences.

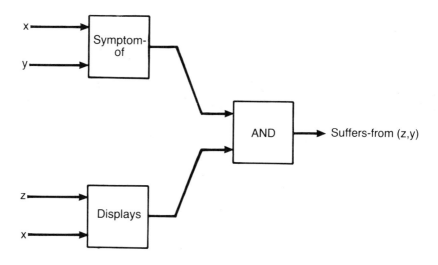

Fig. 5.2 – Dataflow network for Fig. 5.1.

In general a dataflow computer or computer subsystem has three requirements: to store representations of program graphs, to implement some form of data tokens to flow through the graphs, and to provide suitable instruction processing facilities. Each requirement poses certain problems, some of which are quite severe. Program graphs in practice will contain hundreds of thousands, if not millions, of arcs and nodes, and may not always reduce to the neat tree structure shown in Fig. 5.2. Furthermore, if, as is almost certain, the program contains recursive definitions, portions of the structures will be re-entrant. For example, consider the declaration:

If child-of (x, y) or child-of (x, z) and descendant-of
(z, y) then descendant-of (x, y)

(This means that a person x is a descendant of a person y either if x is a child of y, or if there exists a person z such that x is a child of z and z is a descendant of y.) As shown in Fig. 5.3, the graph of this inference needs to replicate itself repeatedly during processing.

Most of the data processed in knowledge-based systems does not consist of single items, but of large structures which would cause unacceptable overheads if they were passed through a dataflow network in their entirety. This problem is being approached by using pointers to the data structures in the dataflow networks, and accessing the structures from fixed memory only when they are required.

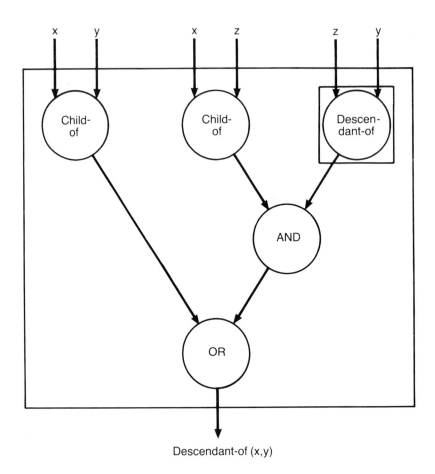

Descendant-of (x,y)

Fig. 5.3 — A recursive graph: the large box needs to be reproduced repeatedly inside the small one.

Three lines of research are being followed in response to these difficulties. The first is to regard a dataflow task as fixed at compile time, and to prohibit re-entrant code. This static approach is illustrated in Fig. 5.4, which uses a network of binary processors each with two alternative output channels. The dynamic approach gets round the problem of re-entrant code by allowing replication of portions of the network at run time. This has the virtue of simplicity, and may become increasingly feasible as hardware constraints slacken. Fig. 5.5 illustrates one possible configuration using this technique (after Tanaka, 1982). The line of development which holds out the most promise in the short term is the tagged system, variations of which are under development at MIT and Manchester University. Each data item flowing through the network carries with it an identification tag, which specifies its type (for example it may be a pointer to a large data structure held in fixed store) and its position in the program. The tags enable data items to be paired and matched with appropriate instructions for processing. The tags also indicate the level of recursion if re-entrant code is used. One node of a data-flow system using this approach is illustrated in Fig. 5.6 (after Gurd, 1982).

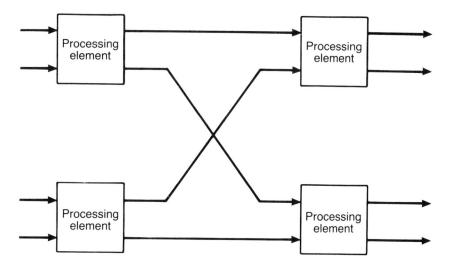

Fig. 5.4 – A static dataflow network (delta network).

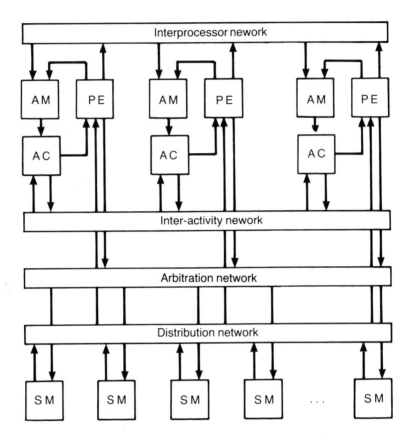

A M Activity memory
A C Activity controller
P E Processing element
S M Structure memory module

Fig. 5.5 — A dynamic dataflow architecture.

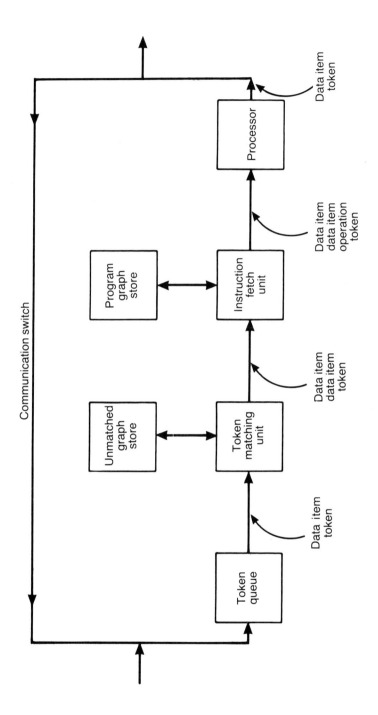

Fig. 5.6 — A tagged dataflow architecture.

5.5 GRAPH REDUCTION ARCHITECTURE

A variation on the dataflow approach discussed above is to evaluate functions by working directly on their graphical representations. As various portions of the graph are evaluated, they are replaced by their intermediate results. In this way the graph is reduced as the evaluation proceeds. As an example, consider again the declaration:

If child-of (x, y) or child-of (x, z) and descendant-of
(z, y) then descendant-of (x, y)

Given the relations:

child-of (Elizabeth, George)
child-of (Charles, Elizabeth)
child-of (William, Charles)

the computation of descendant-of (William, George) unfolds to the graph shown in Fig. 5.7. Evaluation of each of the lowest nodes (which becomes a search to see whether such a node is present in the given relations), can proceed in parallel. The intermediate boolean results are then fed back through the graph as it is reduced, until a single result emerges. The steps are shown in Fig. 5.8.

5.6 ALICE

A computer which incorporates graph reduction directly into its basic architecture is under development at Imperial College, London (Darlington and Reeve, 1981; Cripps, Field and Reeve, 1985). Named Alice (for Applicative Language Idealised Computing Engine), it is one of the first complete fifth generation computer architectures to emerge from the various development teams. It is designed to be programmed in the applicative language Hope (sections 7.7 and 7.8), but can also support declarative languages such as Prolog (sections 7.5 and 7.6).

Given a programming task in the form of a graph of a function, Alice first unfolds the graph by substituting the definition of the function at each node, until the graph is fully computable. It then reduces the graph by computing the value of the function at each node, and substituting this value at higher nodes. See the example in the previous section. Many of the steps of the unfolding and reduction processes can take place in parallel; the architecture of Alice enables the parallel operations to be performed without any explicit instructions from the program.

Step 1:   Descendant-of (William, George)

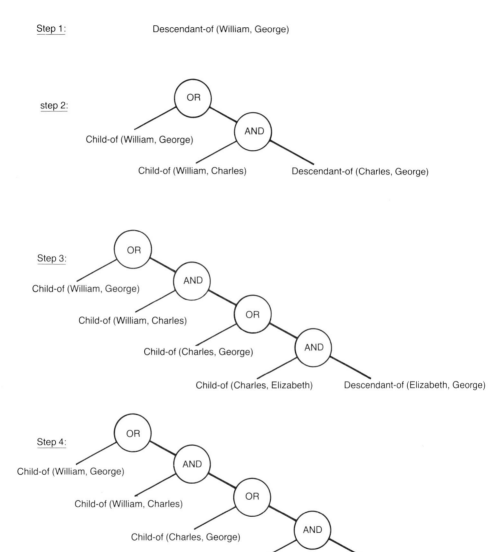

step 2:

OR

Child-of (William, George)

AND

Child-of (William, Charles)   Descendant-of (Charles, George)

Step 3:

OR

Child-of (William, George)

AND

Child-of (William, Charles)

OR

Child-of (Charles, George)

AND

Child-of (Charles, Elizabeth)   Descendant-of (Elizabeth, George)

Step 4:

OR

Child-of (William, George)

AND

Child-of (William, Charles)

OR

Child-of (Charles, George)

AND

Child-of (Charles, Elizabeth)   Child-of (Elizabeth, George)

Fig. 5.7 – Graph of descendant relation: unfolding.

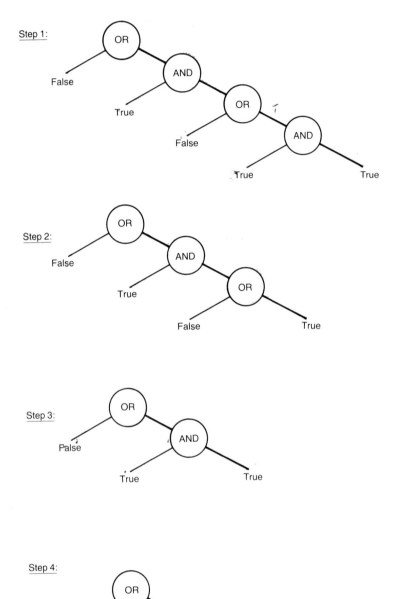

Fig. 5.8 – Graph of descendant relation: reduction.

UNFOLDING

Step 1

P1	Descendant-of	William	George

Step 2

P1	OR	P2	P3

P2	Child-of	William	George

P3	AND	P4	P5

P4	Child-of	William	Charles

P5	Descendant-of	Charles	George

Step 3

P5	OR	P6	P7

P6	Child-of	Charles	George

P7	AND	P8	P9

P8	Child-of	Charles	Elizabeth

P9	Descendant-of	Elizabeth	George

Step 4

P9	Child-of	Elizabeth	George

REDUCTION

Step 1

P2	False

P4	True

P6	False

P8	True

P9	True

Step 2

P7	True

Step 3

P5	True

Step 4

P3	True

Step 5

P2	True

Fig. 5.9 – Alice packets for descendant relation.

Each node in a program graph is represented as a packet within Alice. A packet consists of an identifier field, a function or operator field, and one or more argument fields, which may be data values or references to other packets. There are also control fields used by the computer in its operation. The packets for the above example are shown in Fig. 5.9. Unfolding of the graph of a function is done by a process of pattern matching: the arguments in a function packet are matched against the definition of the packet, and cause the packet to be replaced by further function or operator packets. Reduction proceeds by examination of operator packets: any packet which has all arguments present as values (and not references to other packets) is evaluated and replaced by a packet containing the value of the result. This result is then substituted in all packets which require it, the various control fields in the packet being used for this purpose.

The general layout of an Alice computer is shown in Fig. 5.10. It consists of a large segmented memory serving as a packet pool, and a number of processing agents. The processors and the memory segments are connected by a high-speed switching network which enables any processor to access any memory segment with minimal delay due to other access paths. The configuration chosen is a delta network, comprising a large number of simple switching elements

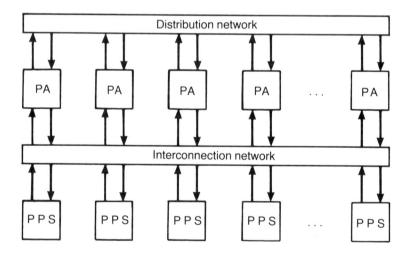

PA Processing Agent

PPS Packet pool segment

Fig. 5.10 — Alice: overall structure.

with four inputs and four outputs in a regular array. (Fig. 5.4 shows a delta network of elements with two inputs and two outputs.) The network operates asynchronously, so that each request for a packet is propagated through the switches as rapidly as possible, and the packet is returned to the processor as soon as the access path is open.

Also linking each processing agent is a low bandwidth distribution network, which contains addresses of processable packets and empty packets. This network includes simple processing elements which transfer these addresses from one processing agent to another, in order to even out the queue of work waiting at each processor. Alice uses the Inmos transputer (section 5.7) as its basic processing element: each main processing agent contains a number of transputers, and additional transputers provide the intelligence in the distribution network.

5.7 THE INMOS TRANSPUTER

An indication of the possible configuration of a fifth generation processing element is provided by the Inmos transputer, which has captured the attention of all the fifth generation development teams. The transputer is designed as a single-chip processing element for parallel computer architectures (Smith, 1983). It has an on-board memory, with high-speed DMA (direct memory access for input and output channels, bypassing the processor) facilities and reception and transmission registers for data transfer between transputers. Its single sequential processor has a reduced instruction set for maximum speed, giving the prototypes an instruction cycle time of 50 nanoseconds. The transputer is designed for a very high throughput of data, even if the processing rate is not so high.

The transputer is designed to be programmable directly in Occam programming language (section 7.4). It is intended to be incorporated in a distributed architecture, with individual transputers connected by a very high speed local area network. As such it is an ideal building block for many components of a fifth generation computer system.

5.8 NON-VON NEUMANN ARCHITECTURES

Since 1946 computers have been based on processing elements which have a single set of registers holding the instructions and data items being processed, and follow a fixed cycle of operations to fetch and execute each machine instruction (section 1.4). This traditional Von Neumann architecture has, by virtue of its simplicity and flexibility, served information technology very well over the years, but the bottleneck created by a single processing cycle and a single set of registers is too restrictive for the fifth generation. However, the potential complexity of VLSI arrays which are not arranged according to simple overall patterns is also to be avoided.

The main line of approach to new chip architectures is to move away from the general-purpose designs of conventional processors, and develop chips which are very efficient at a wide, but specific, range of operations such as pattern matching or searching. The requirements are for a small number of simple basic computing elements, which are replicated a large number of times on the chip. Control paths are to be simple and regular, and extensive pipelining and multiprocessing are to be provided for. A close match is sought between the processing algorithms implemented by the chips and the layout of their circuits (Treleaven, 1983). If these conditions are met, the task of testing the chip, or of proving the correctness of its design, can be applied to each type of processing element rather than the whole chip. The name systolic arrays has been given to special-purpose processing chips of this nature (Foster and Kung, 1980). Applications of systolic array processors include reduced instruction set microprocessors, where each instruction is hardwired into the chip, chips for graph reduction or dataflow operations, chips specially designed for recursive operations and chips which reflect tree structures of processing operations and data.

5.9 INTELLIGENT CAD SYSTEMS FOR VLSI CHIP DESIGN

A major area of research and development in fifth generation hardware is computer-aided design (CAD) systems for VLSI chips. Integrated circuit design is already extensively automated, with facilities for drafting the various layers, building up libraries of functional elements, checking designs against specifications, and simulating the behaviour of a design before fabrication.

What is required for fifth generation computers is even larger and more complex: a hierarchical system which will interact with design engineers at every stage from initial specification to production and design maintenance (Sakamura *et al.*, 1982). The ultimate aim is automatic design compilation, where the logical and performance requirements of a chip are input, and the chip layout is produced, simulated and tested automatically, and then transmitted directly to the chip fabrication equipment. The result is a silicon foundry where the design, prototyping and fabrication cycle is reduced from months or years at present to weeks. A CAD system of this nature is likely to be based on a high-level system design language and standard user interfaces. This is a very ambitious aim, and it is only likely to be fulfilled when fifth generation computers become available. The Japanese approach to this problem is a cyclic one, with intermediate versions of fifth generation computers incorporated into the CAD systems which are used to design the next stage.

5.10 CONCLUSION

Lip service has been paid for many years to the idea of breaking away from the traditional Von Neumann model of computer architecture, but the extent of the innovation has been very small. The requirements of the fifth generation for layers of parallelism, and an emphasis on inference rather than numerical computation look like providing sufficient incentive. Even if the objective of a computer with enhanced intelligence is not attained, the new architectures will provide engines of unprecedented power for conventional computing. The move away from general-purpose processors to aggregations of special-purpose chips is likely to affect all branches of information technology. The increase in the scale of integration, and the advanced CAD systems for microchip production will find applications in every branch of microelectronics. The industrial, economic and political consequences of having access to, or not having access to the new generation of silicon foundries are far-reaching.

REFERENCES

Aiso, Hideo (1982), 'Fifth generation computer architecture', in Moto-Oka (1982), pp. 121–127.

Allen, Jonathan (1982), 'Algorithms, Architecture and Technology', in Moto-Oka (1982), pp. 277–281.

Cripps, Martin, Field, A. J., and Reeve, M. J. (1985), 'The design and implementation of Alice: a parallel graph reduction machine', Department of Computing, Imperial College; reprinted in *Byte Magazine*, June 1985.

Darlington, John, and Reeve, M. J. (1981), 'Alice: a multiprocessor reduction machine for the parallel evaluation of applicative languages', *ACM Conference on Functional Programming and Computer Architecture*, October 1981, pp. 65–75.

Foster, M. J., and Kung, H. T. (1980), 'The design of special-purpose VLSI chips', *IEEE Computer Magazine* **13**, 1, 26–40.

Gurd, John (1982), 'Developments in dataflow architecture', in SPL International, 1982.

Mead, C. A., and Conway, L. A. (1980), *Introduction to VLSI Systems*, Addison-Wesley.

Moto-Oka, Tohru (ed.) (1982), *Fifth Generation Computer Systems: Proceedings of the International Conference on Fifth Generation Computer Systems, Tokyo, Japan, October 19–22 1981*, North Holland.

Sakamura, K., Sekino, A., Kodaka, T., Uehara, T., and Aiso, H. (1982), 'VLSI and system architecture: the new development of System 5G', in Moto-Oka (1982), pp. 189–208.

Seitz, Charles (1980), in *Lambda – the Magazine of VLSI Design*, First quarter.

Sharp, John A. (1985), *Data Flow Computing*, Ellis Horwood.

Smith, Kevin (1983), 'New computer breed uses transputers for parallel processing', *Electronics* **56**, 4, 67–68.

SPL International (1982), *The Fifth Generation – Dawn of the Second Computer Age*.

SPL International (1983), *Fifth Generation World Conference, 1983*.

Tanaka, H., *et al.* (1982), 'The preliminary research on the data flow machine and the data base machine as the basic architecture of fifth generation computer systems', in Moto-Oka (1982).

Treleaven, Philip (1982), 'Fifth generation computer architecture analysis', in Moto-Oka (1982), pp. 265–275.

Treleaven, Philip (1983), 'VLSI processor architectures', in SPL International (1983).

6

Software engineering

Even if the design objectives of fifth generation computers are not achieved, the craft of programming, as practised today, is unlikely to survive for much longer. The writing of programs by conventional methods is coming under pressure from a number of directions. Programs are getting longer: a commercial data processing program is tens of thousands of lines of source code, real-time software is an order of magnitude longer, and fifth generation software will comprise millions of lines. As computer systems take over more and more critical operations, the demands for correctness and reliability of software are becoming increasingly stringent. Software costs have outstripped hardware costs as the major cost element of most computer systems. These pressures converge to a requirement to develop very large, complex software items, which satisfy strict correctness and performance standards, in a controlled, scheduled, budgeted and cost-effective way (Alvey, 1982).

The advent of the fifth generation adds three new dimensions to this problem. Fifth generation software, using artificial intelligence methods to manipulate knowledge, is based on concepts and techniques which are very different from those of conventional data processing. The hardware and software of many fifth generation computer systems are likely to be designed together, with the distinction between the two far more blurred than at present. For this and other reasons it will not generally be possible in most cases to develop fifth generation software on the ultimate host hardware.

The response to these challenges is the evolution of a new profession — software engineering — which will eventually replace programming and probably systems analysis. The end product — computer programs — is the same, but the tools, techniques and outlook are very different from those in vogue today.

6.1 THE SCIENCE OF SOFTWARE ENGINEERING

The term 'software engineering' was first suggested at a Nato conference in 1968. It signifies the development of computer programs in a managed way, subject to strict cost, time and performance constraints (Bauer, 1973; Sommerville, 1982). The term has gradually gained acceptance as the description of a profession standing at the intersection of science and engineering. Software engineering has elements of formal mathematics and logic, computing science, economics and management, as well as a highly developed skill in programming.

Software engineers generally operate in a team environment. The task force for a particular project is divided into small groups, with a management structure often reflecting the structure of the software itself (Babich, 1985). The objective is to reconcile the requirements of the user (or purchaser) of the system with the capabilities of the computing equipment as efficiently as possible. The work is scheduled in advance, budgeted in some detail and subjected to rigorous quality control. High standards of internal documentation are required, as well as compliance with external standards for such things as data communication. The management of a software engineering team poses problems which in many ways are unique: they are a complex blend of technical, administrative, logistical and personal issues which need to be resolved or contained very quickly in order to keep the project as a whole on schedule (Brooks, 1975).

The underlying concepts of software engineering derive from a long-term view of software lifecycles known as software evolution (Lehman, 1980, 1982, 1984). This characterises the various stages of the existence of a software object — design, development, commissioning and then the cycles of use, the detection and correction of errors, and major and minor revisions. Taking this holistic view, and making some attempt to assign costs to the stages, helps to clarify the benefits to be obtained from various techniques of software engineering.

The remaining four sections of this chapter review the four central aspects of software engineering: program structure, program design techniques, proving the correctness of programs and software development environments.

6.2 PROGRAM STRUCTURE

It has now become conventional wisdom that the key to effective software development is very careful design of program structure. The criteria for a well-structured program may be summarised as follows:

- A clear overall structure in terms of modules, with each module carrying out a specific task.
- A clearly defined interface between modules.
- Each module should be a simple combination of the elementary constructions of the programming language.
- It is essential to achieve a high degree of correspondence between the program structure of a module and the structure of the data upon which it operates.
- Each module should leave the data structures on which it operates in a state which is consistent with their defining properties.
- The operation of any particular module should have no side effects — it should not alter any data outside its designated preserve.

These are the ground rules of structured programming; they are much easier to state than to comply with in practice. Successive generations of high level programming languages have incorporated the concepts of program structure to an increasing extent. The trend in languages such as Algol, Pascal and Ada has been to 'seal off' program modules (realised as procedures and functions) to an increasing extent, and to provide strictly defined channels for the passage of data between them. This tendency is taken further in the fifth generation programming language Occam, where each process is designed to be run on a physically distinct processing element.

The requirements of program structure take on another dimension in the context of the development of software by teams of software engineers. The structure of a program must be clear enough so that different portions can be developed independently. Research indicates that the problems of large programs begin at a very simple cutoff point — a large program is a program written by more than one person.

If the ideal of a proper program structure is achieved, a great many benefits accrue. Modules can be kept in libraries for re-use; modules can be tested independently; incorrect or substandard modules can be unplugged and replaced without side effects. These benefits obtain during software development and throughout the cycles of use and revision of software. All the most recent advances in software development environments and program generation tools assume a very strict structure of the software under development. As the idea of integrated hardware and software development becomes a reality, software structure will have to match a further and even more demanding constraint — a close correspondence with hardware structure.

6.3 PROGRAM DESIGN

Program design is a methodology for traversing the long and tortuous path from the initial specification of a program, which is generally vague and incomplete and contains hidden contradictions, to the final code object, which is strictly structured and has passed all the performance tests of developer and user. It is a process of adding detail and precision in an orderly fashion, with equally orderly routes for retreat if parts of the design are leading to dead ends. It is a multi-step process, with each step requiring the input of software developers, users and sometimes independent quality controllers. There are a number of techniques of program design in use at present. Some are fairly informal, and require a straightforward algorithmic approach to the description of a software design. Others are much more formal, with strictly defined program development languages, or diagram conventions in which to express intermediate stages of a design. It is the formal methods which are receiving the attention in the various fifth generation projects, as they seem to have the best chances of being amenable to theoretical proofs of the correctness of modules.

One of the simplest and most popular present-day techniques of program design is stepwise refinement, the name and the method being due to Niklaus Wirth. Stepwise refinement is an algorithmic technique which may best be described in its own formulation:

> State the overall functional steps of a program in a brief, top-level algorithm.

Repeat

Expand each step of the algorithm as a detailed algorithm specifying the steps of its implementation.

Until the task has been specified in sufficient detail for the code of the program to be written.

The emphasis is on top-down expansion, with details added in an orderly manner. The benefits of this technique include its flexibility, its use of a fairly informal notation, and its close links with procedural programming languages such as Pascal and Ada. It is often possible to use the final text of the algorithm as the starting point of the program. The shortcomings of stepwise refinement are that, because of its informality, it does not lend itself easily to formal proofs or checks for correctness at intermediate stages, and, because of its procedural approach, it does not lead naturally to the use of non-procedural programming languages such as Prolog.

A more formal approach, also based on a top-down evolution of program design, is functional decomposition using abstract data types. This approach first identifies the essential abstract properties of the data to be manipulated by a program, and specifies the operation of the program in terms of functions operating on these abstract data types. The functions are defined in terms of more detailed functions as the design progresses, and, at the final stages, 'primitive' procedures are written in order to implement the abstract properties of the data. The benefits of this applicative approach include its rigorous approach to the logical structure of functions and data, and the fact that it is amenable to formal proofs of correctness at all stages. It associates well with applicative programming languages such as Hope (and the Alice graph reduction computer which implements them directly). The disadvantage of the abstract data type approach is that it is very far removed from the surface appearance of a programming task, and from the hardware of most conventional computers. Consequently it is difficult for a non-specialist to understand or check the steps of a program design, and software designed by this technique may not always run very efficiently on present-day computers. However, its rigour and formality make it a very promising candidate for a software engineering approach to fifth generation computing tasks.

A variation on the abstract data type theme is the state machine approach, also known as Parnas's technique. This requires a formal specification of the purpose, exceptions and value(s) returned of each function and operation in a program. The operations and functions are obtained by a stepwise refinement process from a top-level algorithm. The benefit of the method is that the specification of each module is distinct from the procedure for evaluating the module. Accordingly, it is possible in many cases to prove that the algorithm selected for a module satisfies the specification of the module. An approach along these lines is included in the programming language Ada, where each module has a separate specification and code body. The specification describes the interface presented by the module to the rest of the program, and forces all access to the module to be via the specified interface (Barnes, 1982).

6.4 PROVING THE CORRECTNESS OF PROGRAMS

Current methods of program checking involve manual and/or automatic tests of program modules under as many conditions as possible, and comparing the outputs with those expected according to the specifications of the modules. The problem is that, no matter how exhaustive the tests, they can never simulate all the possible permutations of data values and program states. Thus the status of almost every operational computer program is that it is conjectured to be correct, until this is refuted by errors encountered in operation. As programs become orders of magnitude more complex, and are used in critical applications, this approach, no matter how exhaustively applied, will not suffice. What is required is a convincing logical demonstration of the correctness of program modules under all specified conditions of use (Boyer and Moore, 1981).

Techniques of proving the correctness of program modules are still very much in their infancy, and have hardly ever been applied to operational software. However, they are central to the development of credible fifth generation software, and are being actively researched by all the fifth generation development teams. The problem at the current state of development is the limited range of program modules to which formal mathematical proofs can be applied, and the limited number of program languages which lend themselves to any form of automation of the proof process.

A technique which can be applied in some cases is mathematical induction. This first establishes the validity of a proposition in some simple case, such as an empty data structure, and then shows that if the proposition is true in any arbitrary situation, it is also true in the 'next' situation. ('Next' in this context may mean the succeeding value of an integer, or the addition of an item to a data structure.)

For example, consider the data structure known as a list, widely used in artificial intelligence work, which has the cons (construct) operation to add an item at the head of the list. A list has the following minimal defining properties:

> list = empty_list
>> or cons(item, list)
>
> head(cons(item, list)) = item
>
> tail(cons(item, list)) = list

A function append which joins two lists may be implemented by the following module in a Pascal-like programming language:

```
function append(list_1, list_2): list;
begin
    if list_1 = empty_list
        then append:= list_2
        else  append:= cons(head(list_1),
                            append(tail(list_1), list_2))
    end;
```

Consider the proposition that the append function, as implemented above, is associative:

> append(append(list_1, list_2), list_3) =
>> append(list_1, append(list_2, list_3))

The first stage of a proof by induction is to consider a simple case, such as list_1 = empty_list. Using the definition of the append function given in the algorithm for its implementation, the left-hand side of the proposition becomes:

> append(append(empty_list, list_2), list_3)
>
> = append(list_2, list_3)

The right-hand side becomes:

> append(empty_list, append(list_2, list_3))
>
> = append(list_2, list_3)
>
> = Left Hand Side

This establishes the proposition in a simple case. If it is now assumed that the proposition holds for any arbitrary value of list_1, then the requirement is to prove that it is true when an additional item is added to list_1, giving cons(item, list_1). In the latter case the left-hand side of the proposition becomes:

append(append(cons(item, list_1), list_2), list_3)

= append(cons(head(cons(item, list_1)),
          append(tail(cons(item, list_1)), list_2), list_3)

. . . from the definition of append

= append(cons(item, append(list_1, list_2)), list_3)

. . . from the definitions of head and tail

= cons(item, append(append(list_1, list_2), list_3))

. . . from the definitions of append and head.

The right-hand side of the proposition is:

append(cons(item, list_1), append(list_2, list_3))

= cons(item, append(list_1, append(list_2, list_3))

. . . from the definition of append

= cons(item, append(append(list_1, list_2), list_3))

. . . assuming that the proposition is true
for an arbitrary value of list_1.

= Left Hand Side.

Thus the right-hand side of the proposition is equal to the left-hand side for the case of cons(item, list_1) if it is true for list_1. As it has already been established that it is true when list_1 is the empty list, the proposition is true for all values of list_1.

The above simple example illustrates some of the strengths and weaknesses of the inductive method of proving the correctness of program modules. It involves concepts and techniques of formal mathematics which may not be familiar to many programmers. It can only be used with much hope of success on abstract data types with simple defining properties. However, although the proofs can be long and tedious, they are superior to any number of specific tests of the program module with actual data values. This technique, when it can be used, establishes the correctness of assertions about a program module for all possible values of the data items within their specified ranges.

Other techniques of program verification include automatic verification condition generators, which can be applied to languages such as Fortran to produce formal conditions which each module must satisfy in order to be regarded as correct. These conditions are then applied to theorem-proving systems which establish whether or not they are true. Another approach is to use a separate specification language (such as the language Clear) to state the required properties of a module, and to submit its specification to a formal proof process. A third alternative is the use of metafunctions (functions about functions), in order to test the correctness of functional programs. The use of mathematical induction in the example above is a special case of the technique of metafunctions.

Proving the correctness of sequential programs is difficult enough; the problem is compounded when an element of concurrency is introduced. The problem is that classical logic, which underlies program proving, is based on a static environment: assertions are either true or false for all time, and no external agency may alter these values. Concurrency is being investigated by an extension of conventional logic to temporal logic, which allows for the evolution of systems in time (Boyer and Moore, 1981) and by some of the recent developments of alternative systems of logic (Turner, 1984).

6.5 SOFTWARE DEVELOPMENT ENVIRONMENTS

At present the tools available to software developers are an ad hoc collection of compilers, linkers, facilities for maintaining and indexing module libraries, screen design templates and debugging facilities such as tracing, testbeds for individual modules and single stepping through code. Contemporary 'fourth generation' software development tools are various forms of program generators, where a program is entered in a specification language, and the code is generated automatically. These are ideal for certain types of programs, such as question-and-answer training packages, but have limited ranges of application. It is recognised by all the fifth generation development teams that far more powerful software development tools than these will be required to make the cost-effective design of fifth generation software a practical possibility (Hawley, 1986).

What is needed is an integrated programming support environment (Ipse), 'a compatible set of tools based on a methodology for all phases of system development and operation, supporting both technical and management activities' (Alvey, 1982). An Ipse is intended to support software items throughout the entire cycle of design, development, use and maintenance.

The design of an Ipse centres around a database which includes all the modules of all software items under development, as well as module libraries, specifications and intermediate design statements. During the design phase, either of a new program or of modifications to existing software, facilities are needed to check specifications for consistency and completeness, and assist in the proof of assertions concerning the specifications. As modules are specified, and the code written to implement these specifications, facilities are required to test modules individually, and assist in the proofs that their code does implement their specifications.

A matrix of compilation facilities is required, so that the most suitable source code can be used for each application, and modules written in different source languages can be linked in the same program. Program generators are needed for routine aspects such as data file transfer and text screen input/output. A range of target languages is needed to support the various processing elements for which software is being developed. A powerful set of indexing, cross-referencing and linking facilities is required to assist in the assembly of very large programs from all their constituent parts. Finally there is a need for simulators for target processors, so that compiled and linked code can be 'run' with the assistance of tracing, single stepping and other debugging facilities. In this way, many run-time errors can be eliminated before the software is downloaded onto the ultimate host hardware.

The physical realisation of an Ipse is a network of workstations for the software engineers, linked to one or more processing and database management units. Either a local area or a long-distance network can be used. Flexible porting arrangements are required in order to connect various target hardware assemblies or prototypes.

All this is a very tall order, especially since the target hardware is likely to be highly parallel in operation, and the design of hardware and software may be a simultaneous process. It is already obvious that integrated programming support environments will be very expensive to develop and use. Unless some form of timesharing arrangements can be made, their use will be restricted to large organisations, effectively excluding the small-time software developer from participation in fifth generation work.

6.6 CONCLUSION

The slow but steady move from programming to software engineering is likely to be one of the biggest changes in the practice of computing since the development of high level languages. It is beginning to exert pressure on individuals, corporations, educational institutions and nations as the demand for cost-effective development of highly reliable software grows. If information systems factories (Alvey, 1982) for software and hardware development become the norm during the next decade, programmers in the traditional mould may well go the way of car assembly line workers and hot-metal typesetters. Any corporation, institution or nation which is not conversant with the new developments will be relegated to the second division of information technology.

REFERENCES

Alvey, John (1982), *A Programme for Advanced Information Technology*, HMSO.

Babich, Wayne A. (1985), *Software Configuration Management: Co-ordination and Control for Productivity*. Addison-Wesley.

Barnes, John (1982), *Programming in Ada*, Addison-Wesley.

Bauer, F. L. (ed.) (1973), *Software Engineering: An Advanced Course*, Springer Verlag.

Boyer, R. S., and Moore, J. Strother (eds.) (1981), *The Correctness Problem in Computer Science*, Academic Press.

Brooks, Frederick P. (1975), *The Mythical Man-Month: Essays on Software Engineering*, Addison-Wesley.

Hawley, R. (ed.) (1986), *Artificial Intelligence Programming Environments*, Ellis Horwood.

Lehman, Meir M. (1980), 'Programs, life cycles and laws of software evolution', *Proceedings of the IEEE*, **86**, 9.

Lehman, Meir M. (1982), 'Program evolution', Imperial College Research Report DoC 82/1, December 1982.

Lehman, Meir M. (1984), 'Program evolution, programming processes, programming support', Imperial College Research Report DoC 84/1, February 1984.

Sommerville, Ian (1982), *Software Engineering*, Addison-Wesley.

Turner, Raymond (1984), *Logics for Artificial Intelligence*, Ellis Horwood.

7

Fifth generation programming languages

The architecture of fifth generation computers, and their intended range of applications, imply that the programming languages used for fifth generation software will be very different from those in use today. Conventional programming languages such as Fortran, Cobol and Pascal have evolved on the assumption of a computer architecture based on a single sequential processor, and applications requiring data processing. Fifth generation programming languages will have to cope with highly parallel architectures, with different types of processing elements for knowledge base management, inference processing and intelligent interface support, and with applications based on intelligent knowledge-based systems. They will need to be in tune with the philosophy of software engineering, with its requirements for cost-effective, quality controlled code generation, proofs of correctness of code, and software development on integrated programming support environments. Furthermore, fifth generation programming languages require a firm base in the concepts of artificial intelligence, which underlie all aspects of fifth generation computer systems.

The general line of development in programming languages which takes account of these requirements is the range of languages which may be termed non-procedural. Conventional programming languages are procedural: they describe, in exhaustive detail, the steps which a computer must carry out in order to perform a particular data processing task. In other words, they specify to the computer how a particular task is to be performed. They are sequential, and they regard the computer memory as an electronic blackboard, on which information may be written at any time, and existing information overwritten by new values as a computation proceeds. Non-procedural languages are based on a description of what is required of a processing task, and the structure of the data required for the task, but leave to the language processor the details of how the task is to be performed. The distinction between data descriptions and the requirements of a processing task are not always clear-cut, and the properties of the task, as described by the program, are not necessarily interpreted in sequence. Many non-procedural languages are based on the principle of non-destructive assignments: the value of a particular data item, once set, is not altered during the running of the program module in which it occurs. This property is significant if the computer architecture is not based on static memory, but on data flowing from one store to another.

Two types of non-procedural languages are examined in this chapter: declarative languages and applicative languages (although the latter are sometimes regarded as a subset of the former). Also discussed are the artificial intelligence language, Lisp, which has been the starting point for much of the non-procedural language work, and new developments in procedural languages which may make them amenable to certain aspects of fifth generation software.

7.1 LISP

The list processing language, Lisp, originated in 1959 in the artificial intelligence group at MIT under John McCarthy (McCarthy, 1965; Sammet, 1969). It stems from the ideas of Church's lambda calculus (section 1.2), and is intended for problems which involve symbol manipulation and recursion. Most artificial intelligence work falls broadly into this category, hence the popularity of Lisp for these purposes (Narayanan and Sharkey, 1985).

The fundamental data element in Lisp is the atom, which may be an identifier or a number. Atoms are built into lists by the use of brackets. For example, (A B C) is a list of three atoms, and (A (B C) D) is a list containing two atoms and a sublist (B C). The notation (A | B) indicates a list with atom A at the head and the list B as the tail. The data structures built up in this way are termed S-expressions.

Processing in Lisp is in terms of functions written as M-expressions, of which there are five elementary ones:

car[(A B C)] = A   . . . the head of the list
cdr[(A B C)] = (B C)   . . . the tail of the list
cons[(A;(B C)] = (A B C)   . . . the constructor function
eq[(A; A] = T   (for True) . . . equality of atoms
atom[(A B C)] = Nil   (for False) . . . test for an atom

(The function names car and cdr are derived from associated assembly language instructions on the first computer on which Lisp was implemented. They are sometimes re-named head and tail respectively.)

Arithmetic operations are expressed as functions: sum[A; B] gives the sum of the atoms A and B. Arithmetic relations are expressed as boolean-valued functions, or predicates: lessp[A; B] is true if A is less than B. The conditional construction is

[p1 → e1; p2 → e2 ... pn → en]

where p1, p2 ... pn are predicates and e1, e2 ... en are expressions. The construction is scanned sequentially, and the first expression corresponding to a predicate which is true is evaluated. There is also a more conventional if ... then ... else construction, structured as a list:

(if A B C)

If predicate A is true then the value of B is chosen, else the value of C is selected.

The define construction creates new functions, which are then incorporated into the environment of the current program.

A program in Lisp is written as a top-level function which invokes lower-level functions in its implementation. Functions may also be written as S-expressions, enabling them to be processed by other functions, and giving Lisp programs endless possibilities for self-modification. An example of a function written as an S-expression is as follows:

```
(define member (atom_1 list_2)
    (if (consp (list_2))
        (if eq (atom_1 car (list_2))
            T
            (member (atom_1 cdr (list_2))))
        Nil ))
```

The function defined above tests whether atom_1 is a member of list_2. If list_2 is non-empty (checked by the consp function which is pre-defined in most versions of Lisp), then if atom_1 is equal to the head of list_2 then the function is true, otherwise the function is called again to test whether atom_1 is a member of the tail of list_2. In the case that list_2 is empty, the function is false, denoted by the value Nil.

Lisp has been the mainstream artificial intelligence programming language for many years, and almost without exception the AI programs of any significance have been written in Lisp. Lisp has been the starting point for a number of more recent non-procedural programming languages, notably Prolog. Although the 'upper' layers of software of a fifth generation computer are likely to be declarative in nature (see section 7.5), at lower levels there is a need for a procedural language which can operate on large, complex data structures. Lisp, or a derivative of it, is an ideal candidate for this role. One possible evolution of Lisp is into an applicative language (section 7.7), with no destructive assignments, which will bring it into line with dataflow and graph reduction architectures.

7.2 PROCEDURAL LANGUAGES: NEW DEVELOPMENTS

Procedural programming languages in their present form have no place in the fifth generation of computers, but some recent advances, notably the incorporation of parallelism, and the emergence of the language Occam, may mean that the thread of development which started with Algol in 1957 is continued into the computers of the future. As explained in section 5.2, a measure of 'controlled' parallelism can be incorporated into procedural programming languages. This approach was pioneered in concurrent Pascal, and has been incorporated into the real-time language Ada. The most fully developed implementation of parallelism into procedural languages is in Occam, where each module is regarded as a communicating sequential process, which may run on its own, possibly dedicated, processing element. In order to give some details of these developments, the following two sections are devoted to outlines of Ada and Occam.

7.3 ADA

Ada was developed between 1975 and 1980 as a project sponsored by the USA Department of Defense. The final version of the language was written by a team at CII Honeywell Bull led by Jean Ichbiah.

Ada is intended as the primary development language for real-time embedded systems such as missile guidance systems, and is to become the standard language for all such systems for the USA Department of Defense, and possibly those of other Nato countries. It is conceivable that computer systems of this nature will incorporate an increased measure of on-board intelligence as new versions are produced, and thus that Ada may become, by default, a fifth generation programming language.

Ada is a large language, intended for the development of large programs (Barnes, 1982; Young, 1984). It has a number of features to assist in the structuring of programs and data. These include strong data typing, and data abstraction facilities so that the logical properties of a data structure can be separated from its detailed implementation. The concept of generic typing allows the creation of program modules which are independent of the types of data being processed. There are mechanisms for separate compilation of modules, and management of module libraries. There is a tasking mechanism for parallel processing. Ada was designed from the outset for use with a program development environment — the Apse (Ada program support environment).

As an example of a portion of a program in Ada, consider a procedure which collects three incoming signals, and then uses them to carry out some processing task. The incoming signals come from three independent sources, and may arrive in any sequence, serially or in parallel.

```
procedure signal_processing is
    task get_signal_1 is
        entry receive (signal_1: out signal);
    end get_signal_1;

    task body get_signal_1 is
        received_signal: signal;
    begin
        received_signal:=signal_channel_1;
        accept receive (signal_1: out signal) do
            signal_1:=received_signal;
        end get_signal_1;
... similar definitions for get_signal_2 and get_signal_3 ...
    begin
        get_signal_1.receive(sig_1);
        get_signal_2.receive(sig_2);
```

```
          get_signal_3.receive(sig_3);
          process_signal(sig_1, sig_2, sig_3);
     end signal_processing;
```

The three tasks (get_signal_1, get_signal_2 and get_signal_3) are activated in parallel at the start of the procedure. They each call detailed functions (signal_channel_1, signal_channel_2 and signal_channel_3) to receive the signals. Each task then arrives at the receive rendezvous indicated by the entry. . .accept construction. If a task has a signal before the call to the rendezvous in the body of the procedure, it suspends at the rendezvous until the call is reached. In a similar way, if the call reaches a rendezvous before the signal is ready, the calling process waits until the called task has produced the signal. When all three signals have been received, the process_signal procedure is called.

Ada has been widely criticised for its size and the awkwardness of its constructions. Although it is designed to be amenable to formal methods of proving the correctness of program modules, much work remains to be done before this is possible on a wide scale. The unease about Ada stems from the fact that an error in an Ada system could have catastrophic consequences. Nevertheless, the Department of Defense continues to insist on the use of Ada for all future real-time applications. A small number of Ada program support environments are under development, and the experience gained on these will undoubtedly be of benefit to fifth generation software engineering work.

7.4 OCCAM

Occam is a programming language designed to support concurrent processing, in computer systems where many processing elements operate independently but interact (Inmos, 1984). It was developed by Tony Hoare at Oxford University, and is the low-level language of the Inmos transputer (section 5.6). Like Ada, it can be used for real-time embedded systems, but it is much simpler — it is named after the medieval philosopher who pioneered the idea of Occam's razor, a sharp intellectual instrument used to cut away all superfluous details in a system.

Occam is based on the idea of communicating sequential processes (Hoare, 1978). A process performs a sequence of actions, and may communicate with other processes via defined channels. Communication along a channel is synchronous: when both an input and an output process are ready to communicate on the same channel, the data item is transferred, and the processes continue independently. The general concept of communicating processes is illustrated in Fig. 7.1. Data types in Occam are restricted to integers, characters, arrays and strings.

Fig. 7.1 – Communicating sequential processes.

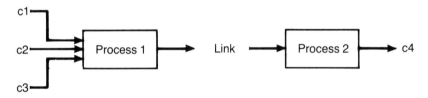

Fig. 7.2 – Hardware configuration for Occam program example.

As an example, consider two simple hardware devices, one of which merges signals from three incoming channels, and the second of which buffers the output from the first, before passing it down an outgoing channel. See Fig. 7.2. An Occam program to control this configuration is as follows:

```
chan link:
par
    while true
        var x:
        alt
            c1 ? x
                link ! x
            c2 ? x
                link ! x
            c3 ? x
                link ! x
    while true
        var x:
        seq
            link ? x
            c4 ! x
```

The two 'while true' constructions operate in parallel as endless loops. Within the first construction, the 'alt' keyword chooses whichever of the three channels is ready for input. The input constructions (c1 ? x, meaning input the value of x from channel c1, etc.) guard their corresponding outputs (link ! x, meaning output the value of x on the channel named link). The second process repeats indefinitely the sequence of input from the link channel and output to c4. Note that the structure of the program is created almost entirely by indentation: the scope of the par, while, alt and seq constructors is the indented lines below them.

The virtue of Occam is its simplicity. It has fewer than thirty reserved words, and only a small number of constructors. Although each process uses destructive assignments, the use of channels for inter-process communication makes it entirely consistent with dataflow and graph reduction computer architectures. Occam was designed with computer architectures of this nature in mind, and with a view to fifth generation applications. It is in tune with the fifth generation philosophy of developing the hardware and software of a computer system together (section 4.5). Together with the Inmos transputer (section 5.7), it provides a modular hardware/ software component of the type which is essential in the construction of highly parallel computer systems. The simplicity of Occam makes it an appealing prospect for proving the correctness of processes. Its lack of data structuring facilities, and closeness to the hardware of the computer system mean that Occam is likely to be the low-level language of fifth generation systems, with applications written in a more abstract language. This is the case with the Alice computer (section 5.6).

7.5 DECLARATIVE LANGUAGES

A language such as Occam represents the idea of procedural programming carried to the frontiers of contemporary computer architectures. Nevertheless it remains a language in the tradition of 'a set of instructions to control the operation of a computer'. It sets out the detailed steps required, in terms of the elementary processing capabilities of the computer, to carry out a task. The artificial intelligence community has been in revolt against this approach for many years: a number of influential practitioners prefer to describe computing tasks in terms of the intrinsic logical properties of the information (or knowledge) and the transformations required on this information

(Kowalski, 1982). This line of research has led to declarative programming languages, of which Prolog is the most prominent example.

The emergence of declarative programming languages has had far-reaching implications. It has enabled the focus of attention to be shifted from the computer to the computing task. It has opened up a wide range of new applications which were previously not regarded as practical propositions for computerisation. These include certain types of expert systems, the new approaches to databases (Kowalski, 1984), the use of logic as a programming approach in education (Kowalski, 1982; Ennals, 1983), and the general problem of inference processing using large bases of knowledge which may be incomplete, imprecise and contradictory. The declarative approach, using Prolog as a starting point, has been adopted by the Japanese fifth generation development group as the basis for their work. The fifth generation kernel language, KLO, used by the Icot team, is based on Prolog (Aiso, 1982).

7.6 PROLOG

Prolog was developed by Alain Colmerauer and his colleagues at Marseilles University in 1972. It is based on the general idea of computation as controlled deduction, and an algorithm as a combination of logic and control (Campbell, 1984; De Saram, 1985). The logic aspect of Prolog is the use of constructions of the form:

A if B and C

known as Horn clauses, where each element is a predicate of the form:

required-for (iodine, thyroid-development)

as introduced in section 2.3. Predicates containing constant data items, as in the example above, are part of the information base used by the program, while those with variables, such as:

causes-deformity(x, y)

are part of the processing task. In this way, both the processing and data structuring aspects of conventional programming are expressed in Prolog in a uniform notation based on logic. The data in predicates can be single items or lists with the same rules for construction as used in Lisp (section 7.1). For example, membership of a list is defined by the clauses:

> member-of(x, (x | z))
>
> member-of(x, (y | z)) if member-of(x, z)

(In other words, a data item x is a member of a list if it is the head of the list or if it is a member of the tail of the list.)

A Prolog program consists of a sequence of Horn clauses containing predicates of the above form, and is activated by queries of the form:

> which(x, causes-deformity(x, stunted growth))   .

An example of a Prolog program which uses a simple chemicals database is as follows:

> elements-of(water, (hydrogen oxygen))
>
> elements-of(ammonia, (nitrogen hydrogen))
>
> elements-of(methane, (carbon hydrogen))
>
> elements-of(carbon-dioxide, (carbon oxygen))
>
> elements-of(alcohol, (carbon hydrogen oxygen))
>
> member-of(x, (x | z))
>
> member-of(x, (y | z)) if member-of(x, z)
>
> component-of(x, y) if elements-of(y, z) and member-of(x, z)

The last clause is interpreted as x is a component of y if y has a list of elements z and x is a member of the list z.

A query such as

> which(y, component-of(carbon, y))

meaning, 'Which compounds have carbon as a component?' produces the results:

> methane
> carbon-dioxide
> alcohol
> no (more) answers.

Processing is done by a process of resolution theorem proving (Robinson, 1965), whereby the Horn clauses are transformed into an equivalent internal format, the predicates 'cancelled out' until either a result is obtained, or a contradiction arises, in which case the query has no replies. In spite of the non-procedural nature of Prolog, the resolution process is sequential, taking the Horn clauses in order of their appearance in the program. This gives rise to a number of problems, in particular relating to 'tight' recursion and the representation of negative information. For example, in most implementations of Prolog, clauses of the form:

linked-to(x, z) if linked-to(x, y) and linked-to(y, z)

and

linked-to(x, y) if linked-to(y, x)

will cause the interpreter to go into an endless loop.

Negation in Prolog is interpreted as a failure to establish that a predicate is true. Thus

not(component-of(x, y))

is true if all attempts to establish

component-of(x, y)

fail. In the words of Robert Kowalski, 'Unfortunately, the implementation of negation by failure makes the success or failure of a negative condition dangerously sensitive to the context in which it is executed' (Kowalski, 1982).

Problems of this nature with the original form of Prolog are being investigated at a number of centres, and attention is focusing on developments arising from this work, which will determine whether logic-based declarative programming languages continue to occupy the centre of the stage in the fifth generation. Recent work includes Parlog, a parallel implementation of Prolog, and various attempts to synthesise elements of Prolog and Lisp, or Prolog and a procedural language. The Icot programming language development plan is for a sequential logic-based language, KL0, followed by a parallel version, KL1, and subsequent versions to match the hardware evolution of fifth generation systems.

7.7 APPLICATIVE LANGUAGES

Applicative languages are a class of programming languages which pre-date fifth generation computers, but which may be drawn into the mainstream of the new generation. They arose in the evolution of ideas of program structuring, and the need for formal procedures of program design and verification. They belong to the class of functional programming languages which has its origins in Church's lambda calculus (section 1.2). They contrast with conventional imperative languages which concentrate on algorithms that determine how a result is to be computed. Applicative languages focus on the actual results of computations, without becoming too involved in the detailed steps of processing. A program in an applicative language is regarded as a set of descriptions of data objects, rather than a set of 'recipes' for obtaining data values.

The defining characteristics of an applicative programming language at first sight seem somewhat restrictive. Programs consist entirely of functions; there are no procedures. Assignments are non-destructive: once a variable has taken on a value, it retains this value for the rest of the module. This means that no two assignments can have the same variable name in the left-hand side. The statements in an applicative language are not to be interpreted in sequence: they are all valid simultaneously. One consequence of this is that there are no loop constructions in an applicative language.

These properties make applicative languages suitable for fifth generation computer development, for a number of reasons. The non-destructive assignments, together with the non-sequential property of statements means that they are ideally suited for data-flow, graph reduction or other parallel supporting hardware archi-tectures. The limitation to functional structure makes programs more amenable to proofs of correctness than would otherwise be the case. The asynchronous interpretation of statements makes the use of special-purpose hardware, with processing elements tailored to certain types of operations, a practical possibility. Some appli-cative languages are based on lists as data structures, placing them in the mainstream of artificial intelligence work.

7.8 HOPE

An example of an applicative programming language is Hope, dev-eloped at Edinburgh University and adopted by the team at Imperial College for the Alice computer (section 5.5). A program in Hope is a function which calls other functions to complete its definition.

Each function describes a data object, which may be an integer, a character string, a list or a more complex structure. A function may be defined for a generic data type, and the specific type passed to it as a parameter. This means that, for example, the same function will sort a set of character strings or a set of numbers. All variables in Hope are local to the function declaration in which they occur; this means that programs are free from side-effects, where one module inadvertently changes the value of a variable in another module. Hope programs are not interpreted sequentially, giving them the mathematical property of referential transparency (Bailey, 1985, 1986). This facilitates the construction and proof of assertions about the correctness of programs, and enables them to be transformed automatically into equivalent forms which are more efficient in their use of the hardware resources of the host computer.

A function in Hope which inserts an element into its proper place in an ordered list is written as follows:

```
dec insert: alpha # list(alpha) → list (alpha)
—— insert  (i, nil)      ⇐ i :: nil;
—— insert  (i, h :: t)   ⇐ if i > h
                            then i :: (h :: t)
                            else h :: insert (i, t);
```

The first line declares a function called insert to operate on a single data item of unspecified type alpha and a list of the same type, producing another list. The second line defines the value of the function given an item i and an empty list as the item i followed by the empty list (the :: notation is equivalent to the Lisp |). The third line defines the value of the function given an item i and a list with a head h and a tail t in two cases: if i is less than h then the function yields the list with head i and tail h :: t; otherwise the head remains h and the function is called recursively to insert i into the tail t.

Whenever this function is called, a process of pattern matching is used to determine which of the definitions is used (both may be tested in parallel). The alternative definitions corresponding to the then and else constructions may also be evaluated in parallel, and the required value selected once the result of the comparison is known. The function is polymorphic, in that it operates on data items of unspecified type (with the restriction that the 'less than' relation holds for the data type).

7.9 CONCLUSION

The main characteristic of the fifth generation programming languages outlined in this chapter is that they are very different from their immediate predecessors. They are non-procedural, non-sequential and non-numeric in emphasis. They will require different programming skills from those practised today, a point with profound consequences for the programming community in every nation with aspirations for a world-class IT industry in the next decade.

At present it is not clear whether Prolog or one of its offshoots will, as widely predicted, become the base language of the fifth generation. This chapter attempts to make the point that there is a wide choice in the matter, and that a number of languages might be used for the various layers of software controlling the processing assemblies which make up a fifth generation computer system.

REFERENCES

Aiso, Hideo (1982), 'Fifth generation computer architecture', in Moto-Oka (1982), pp. 121–127.

Bailey, Roger (1985), 'A short tutorial on the programming language Hope', Department of Computing, Imperial College.

Bailey, Roger (1986), *Functional Programming with Hope*, Ellis Horwood.

Barnes, John (1982), *Programming in Ada*, Addison-Wesley.

Campbell, John (ed.) (1984), *Implementations of Prolog*, Ellis Horwood.

De Saram, Hugh (1985), *Programming in micro-Prolog*, Ellis Horwood.

Ennals, Richard (1983), *Beginning micro-Prolog*, Ellis Horwood.

Hoare, C. A. R. (1978), 'Communicating sequential processes', *Communications of the ACM* 21, 8, 666–677.

Inmos, (1984), *Occam Programming Manual*, Prentice-Hall.

Kowalski, Robert (1982), 'Logic as a computer language in education', in Steels and Campbell (1985), pp. 71–92.

Kowalski, Robert (1984), 'Logic as a database language', Imperial College Research Report DoC 82/25.

McCarthy, John (1965), *Lisp 1.5 Programmer's Manual*, MIT Press.

Moto-Oka, Tohru (ed.) (1982), *Fifth Generation Computer Systems: Proceedings of the International Conference on Fifth Generation Computer Systems, Tokyo, Japan, October 19–22 1981*, North Holland.

Narayanan, A., and Sharkey, N. E. (1985), *An Introduction to Lisp*, Ellis Horwood.

Queinnec, Christian (1984), *Lisp* (English language edition), Macmillan.

Robinson, J. A. (1965), 'A machine oriented logic based on the resolution principle', *Journal of the ACM* 12, 23–41.

Sammet, Jean E. (1969), *Programming Languages: History and Fundamentals*, Prentice-Hall, pp. 405–415 and pp. 589–603.

Steels, L., and Campbell, J. A. (eds.) (1985), *Progress in Artificial Intelligence*, Ellis Horwood.

Young, S. J. (1984), *An Introduction to Ada*, second revised edition, Ellis Horwood.

8

Intelligent knowledge-based systems

Intelligent knowledge-based systems (IKBS), a term coined in the Alvey Report (Alvey, 1982), are the central elements of fifth generation computers. They have been described as 'nearer term applied artificial intelligence' (Taylor, 1983). They correspond roughly to the 'basic application systems' of the Icot programme (Fig. 3.1: Moto-Oka, 1982). Intelligent knowledge-based systems bring together the various hardware and software elements of fifth generation computers in order to achieve the goal towards which all the research and development work is being directed: the use of inference to apply knowledge to perform a task. The success or otherwise of the fifth generation development projects will ultimately depend on whether they lead to the production of useful, cost-effective intelligent knowledge-based systems.

IKBS operate in precisely those 'grey' areas where computers have hitherto been of only limited use. They enter the complex field of human decision making, in order to assist experts such as doctors, geologists, economists and managers in almost every field, and perform functions which were hitherto not possible, such as making tactical decisions during the flight of a missile. They are intended to operate on very large, complex bodies of information and knowledge, and draw inferences based on a combination of hard-and-fast rules, working hypotheses and conclusions inferred from previous operations. People are very good at making calculation plans, but not as good at implementing them: electronic computers are the most recent in a long line of devices to take over calculations from people. Intelligent knowledge-based systems will attempt the same transfer in a much wider field: they will implement the general knowledge processing plans of people or teams of people.

In order to achieve this, an IKBS must have at least the following internal capabilities: classification, concept formation, summarising, abstraction, selection, retrieval filtering, reasoning, planning, modelling, memorising, the formation and use of heuristic ('common sense') rules, and learning. The interaction between an IKBS and the outside world is likely to be via sound, vision and touch, with emphasis on communication in a natural language. This requires the external interaction capabilities of language analysis and production, image perception and generation, and physical object sensing and manipulation (Alvey, 1982). These external aspects of IKBS are discussed in Chapter 9.

The Alvey report identifies a number of potential applications of intelligent knowledge-based systems: scientific diagnosis, database questioning, teaching basic skills, content-determined document retrieval, office scheduling, robot management, picture matching, message interpretation, law consultation, program drafting, technical manual production, industrial process control and warehouse packing. In addition there are military applications, including 'smart' guided missile systems, strategic and tactical planning systems, intelligent communications networks and the potential for use in anti-missile strategic defence systems. Some of these fall into the category of expert systems (section 10.6); others are more general applications of fifth generation computers.

The difficulties of implementing intelligent knowledge-based systems are not to be underestimated. At present the theoretical foundations of the subject are meagre. There is no accepted unit of measurement of knowledge, and no primitive operations on knowledge elements at the same level as basic arithmetic on numbers. In the words of Donald Michie, we need a 'sound and well-quantified theory of knowledge, which at present is next to nothing' (Michie, 1982).

This chapter discusses the approaches and techniques which are being used to realise intelligent knowledge-based systems, and draws attention to some of the problems which are being confronted in the process.

8.1 KNOWLEDGE REPRESENTATION

The key to knowledge processing is knowledge representation – the ability to store large bodies of highly structured information on a computer system in ways which preserve the 'meaning' of the information, and allow it to be processed in all the ways mentioned in the previous section. Knowledge representation is also one of the major challenges to be overcome in fifth generation development work. It is not necessarily amenable to attack by the 'brute force' techniques which sometimes succeed when applied to hardware problems, nor to the highly disciplined minimalist approach which has so often supplied elegant solutions to conventional software and database problems. As discussed in sections 2.2 and 2.3, knowledge is complex, vague, frequently incomplete and can contain contradictions. Most knowledge is a mixture of information and various levels of instructions which control the use of the information. The main dimension of debate about techniques of knowledge representation is concerned with the control aspect: is a single representation structure to contain basic information and the control elements, or are the two to be separated?

A further debate concerns the question of learning. Many AI practitioners are convinced that no system can be described as intelligent unless it has a built-in capacity to learn. Traditionally, there are two approaches to learning – the deductive approach, in which specific knowledge is deduced from general rules, and the inductive approach in which general rules are inferred from specific examples. The problem is to decide which approach, or what combination of approaches, is preferred in each IKBS application, and how to construct mechanisms to implement them.

There are two broad lines of approach to knowledge representation (Steels and Campbell, 1985), termed the declarativist and the proceduralist respectively. The declarativist view is to represent information in a neutral way, independent of its use. Control is achieved at a higher level, by general-purpose knowledge-processing strategies which are applied uniformly to the information. The Prolog language is an implementation of this approach: it forms a knowledge base from associations between items of information and rules of inference operating on these associations, and includes a general theorem-proving mechanism to control the application of the rules to the associations. A variation on the declarativist theme is to include control elements in the knowledge base as distinct entities. The proceduralist approach deliberately blurs the distinction between information and control, and creates representation structures which incorporate both aspects. When the knowledge base is processed, the context of a particular process determines whether information is taken at face value or used for control purposes.

Three specific techniques of knowledge representation are discussed in this chapter: semantic networks, frames and production systems. The fourth common technique, the use of first-order logic, is covered in sections 2.3, 7.5 and 7.6. Three examples of knowledge processing are provided, in order to give some idea of the work involved and the problems to be overcome. They are searching a knowledge base, evidential reasoning and procedural learning.

8.2 SEMANTIC NETWORKS

Semantic networks regard knowledge as a set of associations between concepts (Alty and Coombs, 1984). The concepts are represented as the nodes of a network, and the associations as arcs linking the nodes. Unlike a Prolog program, which lists each association separately, a semantic network can be of any degree of complexity, with many arcs referring to the same node.

Fig. 8.1 illustrates a semantic network to represent the following associations:

> John is a male student who plays football and likes classical music.

> Helen is a female employee who likes football and classical music.

> Joseph is a male employee who plays football and dislikes classical music.

Note that the nodes in the network are all nouns, and the associations are all verbs. The nouns include specific individuals (known as tokens) and general classes (known as types), with a convention of bracketing tokens to distinguish them from types. The verbs include set membership ('is a'), which allows all the operations of set theory to be used on semantic networks. The above is an example of a static semantic network, in which the associations do not alter with time. Dynamic semantic networks can be constructed around verbs as nodes. Fig. 8.2 shows how the following hotel room occupancy record can be represented:

> Mr and Mrs J. Smith stayed in Room 101 from 2nd June 1985 to 13th June 1985.

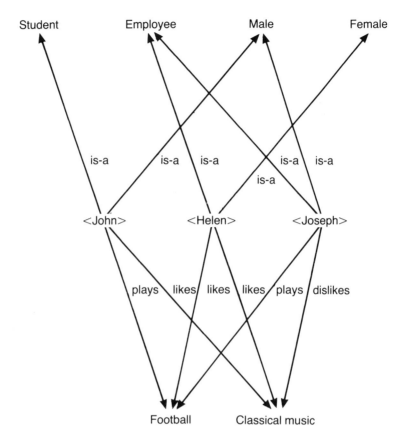

Fig. 8.1 – Semantic network example.

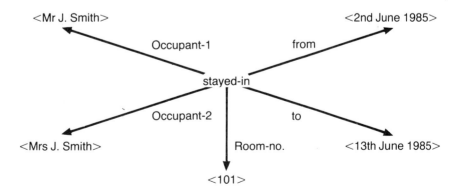

Fig. 8.2 – Dynamic semantic network for room occupancy example.

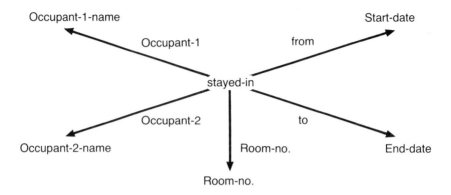

Fig. 8.3 – Prototype semantic network for Fig. 8.2.

Semantic networks can be instantiated from general frameworks, known as prototypes, in which all nodes are types rather than tokens. The prototype for Fig. 8.2 is shown in Fig. 8.3.

The advantage of semantic networks is their flexibility. They can be used for 'pure' information in a declarativist context, or include control arcs and nodes under a proceduralist regime. They are well suited to programs written in Lisp or similar languages. Their structure can be tailored so that information which is required frequently is accessible via short search paths, and items needed less frequently are kept in the background. They have been used to investigate sentence structure, relations between medical symptoms, spatial relationships between objects and symptoms and causes of failure in mechanical devices. The disadvantage of semantic networks is that their potential complexity runs counter to the need for a small number of underlying principles to govern the processing of a knowledge base. Because of their large size and consequent need to be updated in place, they do not lend themselves easily to processing by a dataflow or graph reduction computer.

8.3 FRAMES

The prototype concept used with semantic networks leads to the method of knowledge representation by frames (Alty and Coombs, 1984). A frame is a structure which is instantiated as many times as required in order to link particular data items. A frame has a name, and a set of named slots. Each slot may be filled with a data item, a set of items (known as a unit in this context), or a reference to another frame.

A general frame for the hotel room occupancy example of the previous section is as follows:

Name: ROOM_STAY
         Occupant: OCCUPANT_NAME
         Room_number: Range(1 to 199)
         Start_date: Unit(Day, Month, Year)
         End_date: Unit(Day, Month, Year)

The first slot refers to another frame, shown below. The second slot is filled with a specification of the range of permissible values, and the third and fourth slots have descriptions of the data sets which they are to contain.

Name: OCCUPANT_NAME
         Name_1:   Unit(Title, Initial, Surname)
         Name_2:   Unit(Title, Initial, Surname)

Filled with the data for the specific example above, these frames are as follows:

Name: Room_Stay_8506_09
         Occupant: Occupant_8506_09
         Room_number: 101
         Start_date: 2nd June 1985
         End_date: 13th June 1985

Name: Occupant_8506_09
         Name_1:   Mr J. Smith
         Name_2:   Mrs J. Smith

The frames are given particular identities, and the values of all the data items are filled in.

Frames may also be filled with calls to processing procedures, and the values of data items to be passed to and from these procedures. The above example might be extended to include a call to a procedure which calculates the cost of the stay, given the room number and the start and end dates.

Frames are generally used in a proceduralist knowledge processing context, since they can contain both data and control information, and they can include calls to processing procedures. They are more formally structured than semantic networks, and thus more suited to dataflow and graph reduction architectures. Frames are usually programmed in Lisp, but are eminently suited to processing by functional or applicative languages. The limitation of frames is their fixed structure, which makes the learning aspect of IKBS somewhat difficult to implement with them.

8.4 PRODUCTION SYSTEMS

As discussed in section 2.3, a knowledge representation system requires three levels of data storage: a set of associations between elements forming the knowledge base, a set of rules for drawing inferences from the associations, and a control system for applying the rules in a rational way. A specific implementation of this technique, using first-order predicate logic expressed in the language Prolog, has already been described (sections 7.5 and 7.6). A more general realisation of this approach is by means of production rules, expressed as statements of the form:

if <condition> then <action> .

In general, these rules can be placed in a hierarchy, with the lowest level operating directly on the database, and higher levels of rule operating on lower levels of rule. A variety of control systems can be used, depending on the nature of the knowledge base.

For example, an interactive medical pre-diagnosis system might start with rules of the following nature:

MR1   If specific_question is asked and reply is yes then add question_content to database.

MR2   If symptom_variable described as high or low then measure variable and add reading to database.

R1   If patient_identity not established then establish patient_ identity and read medical_record_summary from disk into database.

R2   If major_symptom not known then enquire major_ symptom and add answer to database.

R3   If temperature > 100 then enquire whether feeling_dizzy.

R4   ...

The first two rules are designated meta-rules MR1 and MR2 since they apply to other rules, and not to data objects. The remaining three rules are at a lower level, and operate on information from or about the patient. A simple control system for a set of production rules such as this might be to examine the rules in sequence from the top, and activate the first one for which the condition is true. When the rule has been applied, and the database updated, the rule set is again examined from the top.

Applying these rules to a patient who has a high temperature and is feeling dizzy, the first pass activates rule R1 to establish the identity of the patient. When the patient's medical records have been read from the disk, the next pass of the rules activates rule R2, to which the reply is 'high temperature'. This activates meta-rule MR2 on the next pass, and the patient's temperature is duly measured. If this is greater than 100, rule R3 is next activated, and the patient replies 'yes' to the question about dizziness. This activates meta-rule MR1 which causes the question content − feeling_dizzy − to be added to the database. And so the diagnosis proceeds.

A production system of this sort lies somewhere between the declarativist and the proceduralist view of knowledge bases. There is a general strategy for applying the rules, which is independent of them, but the rules are organised hierarchically, taking account of the application strategy. This gives great flexibility to the technique, but makes any kind of formal proofs of correctness very difficult. Although the application strategy requires the rules to be considered in sequence, a parallel evaluation of the conditions, and selecting the highest-ranking rule for which the condition is true would be equally effective. The latter lends itself to parallel computation, or some form of grouped evaluation if insufficient processing elements are available for the entire rule set to be examined at once.

8.5 KNOWLEDGE PROCESSING

As mentioned at the start of this chapter, knowledge processing operations include classification, concept formation, summarising, abstraction, selection, retrieval filtering, reasoning, planning, modelling, memorising, the formation and use of heuristic rules, and learning. Most of these are very different from the classical data processing operations of sorting, selecting, storing, retrieving and performing calculations. Two broad categories of knowledge processing operations can be identified. The one group involves the formulation and manipulation of rules. This can be in either of two directions: the deductive, in which new conclusions are drawn from established principles, and the inductive, in which new general principles are inferred from specific evidence. In many applications, it is likely that both directions of inference will be followed. The second group involves searching for a matching (or nearly matching) pattern, or generating and testing alternatives. In practice, search spaces and the number of alternatives to be generated and tested are very large.

There are a number of serious problems to be overcome in knowledge processing, before operational intelligent knowledge-based systems can be constructed. These include dealing with uncertain, incomplete and contradictory information, and preventing combinatorial explosions during processing, in particular during search operations. The first problem is being investigated by the application of 'fuzzy' logic, based on sets which do not have definite boundaries, and by the inclusion of probabilities or weighting factors in inference rules. See section 2.3.

The problem of combinatorial explosions has bedevilled artificial intelligence research for many years. It was one of the main negative factors identified in the Lighthill Report (Lighthill, 1972) which put an end to much of the AI work in Britain during the 1970s. A combinatorial explosion arises when the number of possibilities to be considered in a knowledge-processing operation is orders of magnitude larger than the number which the computer can manage. The point is sometimes overlooked that all computers, including those belonging to the fifth generation, are finite machines — able to store a finite amount of information and knowledge, and able to carry out a finite number of operations in any given time. If an operation is undertaken by a simplistic approach such as trying out all the possibilities, the number to be tested, in practical situations, soon exceeds the capacities of even the largest computers in existence. For example, in a speech recognition system with a dictionary of ten thousand words, an unintelligent search for the meaning of a three-word phrase would have to consider a million million possibilities. The Lighthill report made the very valid point that the number of possibilities to be considered in constrained situations such as chess playing was just manageable by the most powerful computers of the day, but in real-world applications this number would be impossibly large.

The problem of the combinatorial explosion now looks less daunting, for two reasons. On the one hand, the capacities and processing speeds of computers have increased by nearly two orders of magnitude in the last decade, and look set to increase by at least that in the next decade. On the other hand, research into knowledge-processing techniques is concentrating very strongly on intelligent searches, which are able to determine at an early stage whether a particular line of investigation is going to produce a result or not.

8.6 SEARCHING A KNOWLEDGE BASE

As discussed in the previous section, searching a knowledge base and generating and testing a large number of alternatives (which is almost the same process) are fundamental knowledge-processing operations. The field in which the search takes place is known as the state space of the search. The state space may be the contents of a knowledge base, or the set of possible alternatives which can be generated. For example, in a game-playing application, the state space is all the possible moves in the game. The most common structure of a state space is a tree, spreading from the root representing the start (or current) state of the system, and branching for each possibility at each subsequent stage. The final states of the system represent the goals towards which actions are directed. An example of a state space in a tree structure of this sort is shown in Fig. 8.4. It represents the possible configurations of a certain microcomputer system.

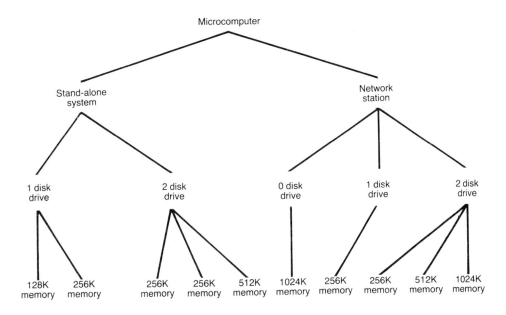

Fig. 8.4 — A state space as a tree structure.

Depending on the circumstances, there are two possible directions in which a tree can be searched. Forward-chaining involves moving from the current state at the root of the tree towards a goal state which must satisfy some conditions. Backward-chaining starts at the goal state and determines which path must be selected at each node in order to achieve this goal. In a game-playing application, forward-chaining is used to investigate alternative moves starting at the current state of the game, whereas backward-chaining is used to determine what sequence of moves will lead to some specific goal state of the game.

Whichever the direction of the search, there are two strategies which can be used. The depth-first strategy considers all the possible consequences of each move at each state, before considering an alternative move. The breadth-first strategy considers all possible alternatives at each state, before considering the consequences of each one. The two strategies are illustrated in Fig. 8.5. Much current research is aimed at increasingly intelligent control strategies for searches, in order to avoid the dangers of a combinatorial explosion. Some measure of the value or benefit (or hazard) of each intermediate node of the state space is computed before any subsequent nodes are investigated. The processing time and effort spent on these intermediate evaluations is proving to be worth the effort in view of the reduction in the size of the space to be searched. Most contemporary approaches are a combination of breadth-first and depth-first searches.

8.7 EVIDENTIAL REASONING

An example of the type of knowledge processing which will be undertaken by fifth generation computer systems is drawing conclusions from evidence. A body of evidence, such as that given at a trial or an enquiry into some incident or proposed development, is often very large, and may be inconsistent, incomplete, biased or deliberately misleading. Furthermore, the evidence is presented in a variety of forms, such as transcripts of cross-examination, tables of figures including speculative projections, photographs, maps, diagrams and scientific and forensic results.

The problem facing researchers is to assimilate a very large body of knowledge of this sort, assign relative weights to items, resolve inconsistencies and draw conclusions, or at least reach some consensus view of the situation described by the evidence. The traditional

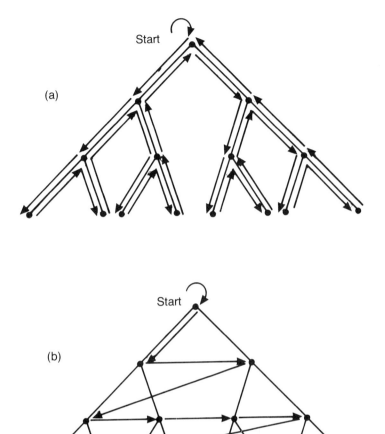

Fig. 8.5 — Depth-first (a) and breadth-first (b) searches of a state space.

approach to processing uncertain data of this sort is Bayesian probability models, in which the probability of conclusions drawn from
items of evidence can be calculated by assigning probabilities to the
original items of evidence. An alternative approach (Lowrance and
Garvey, 1982) currently under investigation is to develop a mathematical theory of evidence, and use it to arrive at consensus opinions
from bodies of evidence, and to draw conclusions from the opinions.
It requires a mechanism for deriving meaning from passages of
natural language, and then processing the meaningful statements in

a systematic way in order to resolve inconsistencies and draw con-clusions. This approach is still very much in its infancy, but it is a good example of the direction in which intelligent knowledge-based systems are evolving.

8.8 PROCEDURAL LEARNING

The concept of procedural learning (Langley, 1985) has its roots in observations of the way people learn. When confronted with a particular type of problem for the first time, a person has only weak, general methods of approach, including trial-and-error and heuristic approaches. In terms of the searching strategies discussed above, the person has no method of evaluating intermediate nodes in a search, and must therefore try a very large number of possibilities before arriving at a solution. As the person gains experience and expertise, more powerful analytical tools are developed, enabling the search to be narrowed down very quickly. For example, a doctor with many years of experience can generally arrive at a diagnosis with a very small number of questions to or tests on a patient.

Procedural learning is an attempt to transfer to computer systems this process of evolving search techniques from experience. An IKBS using the technique requires a number of interacting facilities. These include the ability to generate alternatives in any given situation, and the ability to evaluate results. There is a causal attribution system which is able to determine which choices or activities are responsible for an improvement or degradation of the solution process, and an ability to modify the problem-solving strategies with the benefit of hindsight. Using these techniques, a procedural learning system is able to solve problems from the outset, at first by 'brute force and ignorance', but with reflection on its actions during each attempt, and incorporation of its experiences into its operational strategies. As more instances of the problem are solved, the strategies become more efficient, and the magnitude of the tasks which can be under-taken is increased.

The knowledge in a procedural learning system is generally expressed as production rules. The system is set up with very weak, general rules, and derives more specific and powerful sets of rules as it is used. Rules are postulated and then retained or discarded, depending on their effects on the performance of the system. The rules are arranged hierarchically, and thus include an element of control over the way in which they are applied. The self-assessments carried out evaluate the validity of the specific rules as well as the meta-rules which govern their application.

For example (after Langley, 1985), given an algebraic equation such as

$$3x - 4 = 17$$

to solve, an early set of rules derived by a procedural learning system is as follows:

>If function_1 has an argument num_1
>and function_2 is the inverse of function_1
>
>then apply function_2 to both sides of the equation
>with num_1 as its argument.

In the above formulation, num_1 represents a number and not an unknown in an equation. Applied to the above equation, the rule notes that the left-hand side includes the function $f(y) \rightarrow y - 4$, and therefore applies the inverse function $f(z) \rightarrow z + 4$ to both sides. However, it could equally well have noted that the left-hand side includes the function $f(w) \rightarrow 3w$, and applied its inverse, $f(v) \rightarrow v/3$, which would not have led to a solution at the first step. After further trials and errors, and several sets of production rules which are deficient in some way, a set which works in all cases is derived:

>If function_1 is at the outer level of the equation
>and function_1 has argument num_1
>and function_2 is the inverse of function_1
>
>then apply function_2 to both sides of the equation
>with num_1 as its argument.

Once the system has derived the above rule set, which is applied repeatedly to an equation until a solution is produced, it obtains the correct solution to all equations of the above form at first attempt.

8.9 CONCLUSION

Intelligent knowledge-based systems are the central challenge facing the fifth generation development teams. Although demonstrator IKBS implementations can be produced at intermediate stages, it is only when the advanced hardware and software systems become available that fully operational versions will be possible. The Alvey programme (Alvey, 1982) has been scheduled to take account of this, and plans a number of small- and medium-scale IKBS demonstrators to act as feasibility studies, and to promote interest in the type of products that will be possible through intelligent knowledge-based systems. At the same time it is concentrating on building up an infrastructure of IKBS practitioners in Britain, and promoting basic research, a large amount of which is needed before the implementation stage is reached for full-scale intelligent knowledge-based systems. The Icot approach to IKBS (Furukawa, Nakajima *et al.*, 1982) is firmly centred on logic programming as the basis of knowledge representation and processing systems and the meta-inference systems which will control them. A cyclic development path is proposed, with new IKBS versions developed to coincide with advances in hardware and software. One of the first applications of each IKBS realisation is to assist in the development of the next version of its own hardware and software support systems.

REFERENCES

Alty, J. L., and Coombs, M. J. (1984), *Expert Systems: Concepts and Examples*, NCC Publications.

Alvey, John (1982), *A Programme for Advanced Information Technology*, HMSO.

Furukawa, K., Nakajima, R., Yonezawa, A., Goto, S., and Aoyama, A. (1982), 'Problem solving and inference mechanisms', in Moto-Oka (1982), pp. 131−138.

Langley, P. (1985), 'Strategy acquisition governed by experimentation', in Steels and Campbell (1985), pp. 52−68.

Lighthill, James (1972), *Artificial Intelligence: Report to SERC*, HMSO.

Lowrance, J. D., and Garvey, T. D. (1982), 'Evidential reasoning: a developing concept', *Proceedings of the International Conference on Cybernetics and Society, Seattle, 1982*, pp. 6−9, IEEE.

Michie, Donald, 'Aspects of the fifth generation: the Japanese knowledge bomb', in SPL International (1982).

Moto-Oka, Tohru (ed.) (1982), *Fifth Generation Computer Systems: Proceedings of the International Conference on Fifth Generation Computer Systems, Tokyo, Japan, October 19−22 1981*, North Holland.

SPL International (1982), *The Fifth Generation — Dawn of the Second Computer Age*.

Steels, L., and Campbell, J. A. (eds.) (1985), *Progress in Artificial Intelligence*, Ellis Horwood.

Taylor, J. M. (1983), 'Intelligent knowledge based systems: a programme for action in the UK', Science and Engineering Research Council/Department of Industry IKBS Architecture Study.

9

Intelligent user interfaces

The significantly increased intelligence of fifth generation computers is not intended to remain hidden in the depths of their inference and knowledge base processing mechanisms. One of the main aims of the fifth generation development programmes is to raise the level of interaction between computer and user to something approaching the intelligence inherent in interpersonal communications. What is required is far more than the rather shallow concept of 'user friendliness' which has been the best that conventional computers have aspired to (but seldom achieved). Fifth generation computers need a 'cognitive compatibility' (Michie, 1982) with their users.

There has always been a very wide gulf between the way computers process information and the way people think. Fifth generation computers will narrow this gulf a little, but it will still remain a significant divide. The current state of affairs concerning the interface between a computer system and the person using it may be described in Fig. 9.1. The boundary between computer and user is very close to the way the computer operates, and consequently it requires a lot of effort on the part of the user in order to establish communication with the computer. Put another way, contemporary user interfaces require users to do their best to think like computers. Intelligent user interfaces, as shown in Fig. 9.2, are attempting to

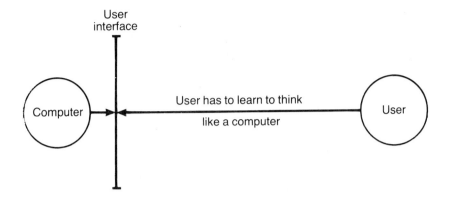

Fig. 9.1 — A contemporary user interface.

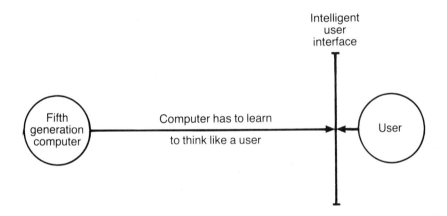

Fig. 9.2 — An intelligent user interface.

build 'knowledge-based bridges' between 'partners which are intrinsically incompatible' (Michie, 1982). They require far less effort by the users to come to terms with the computers, but in order to achieve this, the computers must do their best to think like their users. This is no mean task.

One of the main reasons for the emphasis on intelligent user interfaces is that fifth generation computers are intended to be used by very large numbers of people, the majority of whom are not computer specialists. Fifth generation computers are intended for offices, shops and factories, as well as the workplaces of scientists, engineers, doctors and other specialist professionals. In Japan the

social requirements of the new generation of computers are para-
mount, and are an intrinsic part of the overall social policy for the
country during the next few decades.

9.1 COMPUTERS AND THEIR SYMBOLS

People communicate, amongst other ways, by means of visual and
verbal symbols, which have various shades of meaning according to
the context of the interaction. The relationship between concepts
and their realisation in communicable symbols is a fundamental
aspect of human psychology, and has been the subject of study for
many years. Contemporary computer interfaces concentrate on a
very small subset of these symbols: numbers or graphs of numbers,
technical diagrams, individual words in a control context, and
extended passages of words as data, which are recognised by a user
as natural language but not by the computer. Simple icons are
beginning to be used as control symbols. At present, output from
computer to user is generally confined to printed or displayed
symbols, and input from user to computer to pressing buttons for
a fixed set of symbols, such as on a keyboard.

Fifth generation user interfaces are setting out to broaden the
scope of this symbolic interaction very considerably. For each
particular application, the user interface is to be an intrinsic part
of the system as a whole, using the form of communication with
the user which is most appropriate. For example, intelligent robots
are likely to have some measure of visual discrimination, as well as
a sense of touch. Both senses will relate to the robot's perception of
the three-dimensional space in which it operates. A big advance is
expected in communication with words between user and computer,
both spoken and written. In order to deal with the human aspects of
user–computer interaction, psychologists and linguists are working
with computer scientists in the design of the new generation of
interfaces.

In order to provide the depth of intelligence, and the close links
to the intelligent knowledge-based systems required by fifth generation user interfaces, a great deal of hardware and software support
is needed. The various layers of the intelligent interface support
mechanism in the Japanese fifth generation computer model are
shown in Fig. 4.1. In most cases these will amount to large, semi-
autonomous knowledge processing systems in their own right. In
addition to the custom VLSI chips needed for the support mechanisms, a variety of new hardware devices will be needed for the

'surface' of the interface: high-resolution flat screen displays, video cameras and projectors, infra-red sensors, sophisticated sound synthesisers, etc.

9.2 FOURTH GENERATION INTERFACES: WIMPS

Some idea of the trend towards intelligent user interfaces can be gained by examining the current range of fourth generation interfaces which are beginning to come into use. They are aimed at improving the conceptual communication between user and computer at a visual level, and reducing to a minimum the amount of keyboard control that is needed to operate a program. They allow computers to be used in a much more flexible manner than before, and reduce the dominance of traditional keyboards as a means of input and control. The mechanisms are collectively known as Wimps: for windows, icons, mice and pointers.

Windows — portions of the display screen used for different tasks from the rest of the screen — allow a computer to appear to be doing more than one task at once. Many tasks carried out by users do not fit neatly into the categories of computer software currently available, such as word processor, spreadsheets and database management packages. For example, a user may need to make notes based on the figures in a spreadsheet: the required portion of the spreadsheet can be displayed in a window while the user enters notes using the word processor.

Icons are an attempt to move away from the dominance of the written (or displayed) word for the control of programs. Instead of a word, or a cumbersome phrase in computer jargon, the user is presented with a range of simple pictures showing the control options. For example, instead of the phrase 'Delete file', the user is shown a picture of a file and one of a waste paper basket. The use of icons makes a program independent of any particular language, allows some programs to be used by people who are illiterate, and helps to improve the cognitive compatability between users and computers.

The mouse is a complementary control device to the icon. It enables programs which use icons or similar control configurations to be operated without a keyboard. The user moves the mouse across a flat surface, causing a pointer or highlight to move in a corresponding way on the display screen. Pressing a button on the mouse activates the choice indicated by the pointer. The combination of mouse, pointer and icon provides a control mechanism which is far closer to the way most people think than the rather sterile, jargon-laden 'dialogue' with its limited, fixed control paths which is now being superseded.

These fourth generation interfaces are a big step forward, and are the first sign that the human side of person-to-computer inter-action is getting serious attention. Fifth generation interfaces, with their roots in natural language and artificial intelligence, will require an even bigger advance.

9.3 SPEECH SYNTHESIS AND VOICE RECOGNITION

The use of the spoken word for the interaction between a computer and its user is one of the main specific goals of the fifth generation computer programmes. Although it is a totally different problem, it is closely associated in practice with natural language recognition, which is discussed in the next section. If a sufficient level of success in these areas is achieved for a wide range of applications to become possible, then great benefits will follow. However, the difficulty of the task is not to be underestimated. The English language contains a great number of pairs or triplets of words which sound alike but have very different meanings. In other languages, notably Chinese, the problem is even worse. To illustrate this point, an eminent Chinese linguist has written a text in which every word is pronounced almost identically. Once the barrier of word recognition from sound has been passed, the problem of interpreting the word in its context remains.

The principles of representing a sound signal in digital form are well known. The accepted mechanism is to sample the sound wave at regular intervals, measuring its amplitude, and transform the sequence of numbers obtained into another set of numbers which indicate the strengths of the various frequencies making up the sound. The technique of Fourier transformation is used. A relatively pure note, such as the sound of a flute, is predominantly a single frequency, with a small number of higher frequencies or harmonics. A spoken word, however, is a complex mix of frequencies, each persisting for a short period of time. Variations of pitch, accent and emphasis make it difficult to establish an accepted digital template for spoken words. If the encoding or decoding of the speech signal is to take place in real time, considerable processing power and computer memory are required. For example, more than one hundred kilobytes of data are needed for one second of high-quality sound.

Speech synthesis — the production of words or extended passages in a natural language by a computer − is a simpler task than its converse, voice recognition. The fundamental mechanisms for speech synthesis from text stored in character form are already fairly well established. Groups of characters are interpreted by the speech synthesis system as allophones − the basic ingredients of spoken words. The digital representations of the sounds of these allophones are retrieved and placed in sequence. They are then passed through a smoothing process in order to run the syllables naturally into one another, before being decoded into an analogue representation of speech, ready for transmission. A three-tiered speech synthesis system developed by Digital Equipment Corporation (Bruckert *et al.*, 1983) follows this approach. At present work is concentrating on improving the somewhat limited vocabulary of speech synthesis systems, and dealing with the shortcomings such as lack of natural rhythm and phrasing. Variations in pitch, tone and accent are also being introduced.

Voice recognition is a problem which is going to stretch fifth generation computers to their limits. It calls for every aspect of the hardware and software of a fifth generation computer in order to take a stream of incoming continuous speech and, in real time, decode and interpret it. A number of voice recognition projects have already been undertaken, for example the Darpa Hearsay II speech understanding system (Erman *et al.*, 1980) and the Logica Logos system, but without any great measure of success. All that has been achieved is the recognition of a limited vocabulary of words and phrases from a known speaker, whose voice has been 'learned' by the computer system.

It is becoming fairly clear that a pipelined approach to voice recognition is required, with stages to filter out the noise and speech characteristics peculiar to the individual, recognise the 'pure' speech elements and interpret these as syllables, words, phrases and sentences. At each stage, a high level of parallel processing is required, in order to investigate a number of possible interpretations simultaneously. Recognition of continuous speech and interpretation of natural language are closely linked, and the 'clues' provided by the interpretation mechanism are vital in the recognition process. Most sounds can be recognised with any measure of certainty only if their context is known (as sometimes happens with human speech); a cyclic approach may be needed in order to hypothesise a recognition of syllables into words and then check whether a meaningful context is established.

9.4 NATURAL LANGUAGE RECOGNITION

The background to the work in natural language recognition is discussed at some length in section 2.6. The two aspects of the problem dealt with in that section are syntax — the recognition of linguistic structures — and semantics — the search for meaning. Current research into natural language recognition is adding a third contextual layer, referred to as scripts in some of the work (Hendrix and Sacerdoti, 1981). This approach recognises that language recognition cannot take place in a completely open-ended situation, and that each computer application which interacts with its users via natural language operates in a particular context. Scripts or similar constructs define the overall parameters of the context, and allow meanings of statements to be derived in relation to these contexts. For example, an intelligent database used for criminal investigations has a particular context, and all statements made either by the computer or by its users are in terms of this context.

Natural language recognition is a task well suited to almost every aspect of fifth generation computer development. Both the syntax and the semantics of natural languages can be expressed in terms of logical rules, making them amenable to programming in a logic-based language. The Icot team is following this approach in their work on natural language recognition (Yasukawa, 1983). At both syntactic and semantic levels, much of the processing involves high-speed searches of large knowledge bases. This is an operation ideally suited to parallel processing using loosely coupled processors in a dataflow or graph reduction architecture. At a lower level, the pattern-matching operations can best be carried out by custom VLSI chips (Allen, 1983). Accordingly, it is now possible to envisage a natural language recognition engine constructed from these hardware and software elements, forming the intelligent user interface mechanism of a fifth generation computer system. However, the assembly of such an engine is scheduled as the final stage of the Japanese fifth generation programme, and is unlikely to be achieved earlier by any of the other development teams.

As work on natural language recognition and processing proceeds, a number of researchers are beginning to sound notes of caution (for example, Kaplan and Ferris, 1982). They point out that natural language may not be as effective a means of communication between user and computer in many situations as it has been thought to be. Natural language is very rich and subtle, and can convey meaning at a number of levels simultaneously. However, it can also be vague, ambiguous, incomplete and inefficient. Many commentators have

paid lip-service to the idea of natural language as the ultimate programming language, but this runs counter to the move towards more
precisely defined functional languages described in Chapter 7. The
problems of proving the correctness of a program stated in a natural
language (which will require the proof itself to be in a natural
language) are almost certainly insurmountable.

The most likely outcome of this is a compromise among a
number of factors. On the one hand it is unlikely that any computer
system will be able to cope with the full range and complexity of a
natural language in its totality. But once a certain threshold is
passed, the subset which can be dealt with will be large enough to
be useful in a wide variety of situations. On the other hand these
constraints can possibly be put to creative use in each application
by providing limits on the possible interpretations of any statement,
and helping to avoid nonsense being assimilated into a knowledge-
based system. The verbal exchanges in a great many situations are in
terms of a precisely defined subset of natural language: surgical
operations, stock market transactions, air traffic control, piloting a
ship or submarine and most training situations are a few obvious
examples. It is quite conceivable that a fifth generation computer
system will be able to come to terms with the subset of the language
used in the particular context.

9.5 IMAGE PROCESSING

Image processing is regarded as an essential interface technique for a
number of fifth generation applications, notably intelligent robots,
smart guided missiles, remote-controlled surface exploration vehicles
for distant planets, intelligent CAD systems, applications using maps
and a variety of medical applications. As in the case of voice recognition, it is unlikely that the human level of performance will be
attained: the human eye has 120 million rods, 6.5 million cones and
1 million strands in the optic nerve (Duff, 1982). The aim of the
fifth generation development teams is to develop image-processing
systems which are sufficiently discriminating to be of use in the type
of applications mentioned above. The background to the work in
image processing is described in section 2.7.

The objective of image processing is to 'recognise' the objects
present in a visual display such as that presented by a video camera,
and to generate images of similar quality and realism. As in the case
of speech recognition, image processing operates at several levels.
At the lowest level is a means of identifying various zones of an

image as belonging to particular shapes. The intermediate levels are concerned with identifying shapes as recognisable objects, and the top level refers to a knowledge base containing significant properties of the shapes in order to process them as required.

Most research into image processing is concentrating on the development of special-purpose hardware, in particular for shape recognition and generation. The line of approach which seems most promising is to construct an array of special-purpose processing elements, one for each pixel of the display. The processors are all connected to their eight immediate neighbours, as well as to the overall control mechanisms. See Fig. 9.3. A television-quality image will require approximately 1 million of such processing elements; current systems used for research make do with far fewer, for example the Clip4 system at London University (Duff, 1982) uses an array of 96 by 96 processors. Variations on the cellular logic approach include systolic arrays (section 5.8) of pipelined processors, which are not as closely coupled, and operate with a greater degree of autonomy. A promising technique for the generation of realistic images is the use of a class of mathematical functions known as fractals. These take a basic shape and replicate it in smaller and smaller versions within itself. With slight perturbations, fractals produce shapes and textures which closely resemble the surfaces

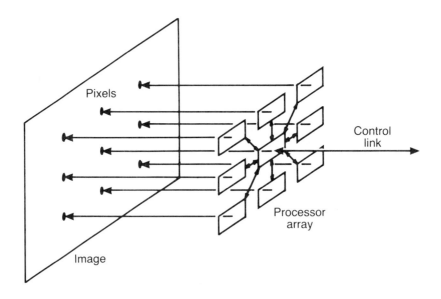

Fig. 9.3 — An array of image processors.

and outlines of natural objects such as mountains, clouds and bodies of water.

The top level of image processing referred to above requires a cognitive framework for the representation and processing of visual symbols. This establishes a context for the more detailed image-processing operations, and an image-representation structure for the knowledge base which will accompany each application. At present there is no wide agreement on the way such a framework should be constructed. One line of development is using the architecture of the human visual cortex as a model (McCormick *et al.*, 1982). If this development is successful, it may be applicable to other fields of artificial intelligence.

9.6 THE PSYCHOLOGY OF HUMAN—COMPUTER INTERACTION

Behind the new techniques of human—computer interaction should lie a body of knowledge which describes the psychological framework within whcih such interactions take place. It is indicative of the engineering approach to computing that has prevailed for the last forty years that no such body of knowledge exists at present. However, the balance is now being redressed with research under way at a number of centres in order to investigate the aspects of human behaviour which are relevant to the interaction between a computer and its user. Most of the fourth generation user interfaces described in section 9.2 are results of early stages of this work.

The most obvious problem is the cognitive mismatch between user and computer which has existed since the first computers were programmed and operated by connecting plugboards. Four major aspects of this problem have been identified (Harris, 1982): the language problem, problems caused by the conceptual viewpoint of the user, the problem of steering through the control paths of a program, and the differences between the user interface philosophies of different software packages. The language problem is due, amongst other things, to the jargon of computer systems designers being used in user interfaces, and the particular use of natural language that has grown up within the computing community (the classic example being multiply-compounded nouns used as adjectives: 'high resolution graphics system memory overflow error address' is one fairly straightforward example). Although the situation has improved a lot in recent years, the control paths in many programs are long and tortuous, and it is quite easy for a user to become hopelessly lost.

Furthermore, many programs have no simple escape mechanism. The differences in user interface philosophy between programs is being countered to some extent by integrated ranges of software packages, and by the insistence of hardware manufacturers that all software on their computers conforms to certain principles of user interface.

Two lines of research currently being undertaken should be of great help in the design of intelligent user interfaces. One is an attempt to identify those communication skills which make some human experts very effective at communicating their expertise to others. If it proves possible to incorporate some of these communication skills into the design of fifth generation user interfaces, or the philosophies behind the designs, then the quality of these interfaces will be greatly enhanced. The other line of investigation is an analysis of human behaviour in complex problem-solving situations: what blend of deductive, inductive, lateral, heuristic or inspirational mental effort is actually brought to bear when an expert sets out to solve a complex task? Once some answers to this problem are known, and they will no doubt vary from one field of expertise to another, serious attempts can be made to reduce the cognitive mismatch between user and computer.

9.7 CONCLUSION

In many ways the success or failure of the fifth generation computer initiative depends on the progress made in intelligent user interfaces. Fifth generation computers are not intended to usurp human intelligence, but they require a means of communication with their users at a higher level than at present, in order to make their intelligence accessible and productive. Establishing communication at the right level between a computer and its user is an essential and integral part of intelligent knowledge-based systems. Fifth generation computers are not intended to be the preserve of the privileged few; they are intended to bring the benefits of advanced information technology to large numbers of people in all walks of life, in all countries. This social aim is explicit in the Japanese fifth generation programme, and is essential for the continued viability of computer manufacturers and systems designers worldwide, as they depend to an increasing extent on sales of their products to a broad market. If they are not readily accessible and easy to use, computers with enhanced intelligence could well become objects of suspicion and fear, or they could simply be ignored by large numbers of potential users.

REFERENCES

Allen, J. (1983), 'VLSI applications: speech processing', in Scarrott (1983), pp. 41–48.

Bruckert, E., Minow, M., and Tetschner, W. (1983), 'Three-tiered software and VLSI aid developmental system to read text aloud', *Electronics* **55**, 8, 133–138.

Duff, M. J. B. (1982), 'Parallel architecture and vision', in SPL (1982).

Erman, L. D., Hayes-Roth, F., Lesser, V. R., and Raj Reddy, D. (1980), 'The Hearsay II speech understanding system: integrating knowledge to resolve uncertainty', *Computing Surveys* **12**, 2, 213–253, June 1980.

Harris, L. (1982), 'The four obstacles to end user computer access', in SPL International (1982).

Hendrix, G., and Sacerdoti, E. (1981), 'Natural-language processing: the field in perspective', *Byte* **6**, 9, 304–352.

Kaplan, S. J., and Ferris, D. (1982), 'Natural language in the DP world', *Datamation* **28**, 9, 114–120.

McCormick, B. H., Kent, E., and Dyer, C. R. (1982), 'A cognitive architecture for computer vision', in Moto-Oka (1982), pp. 245–264.

Michie, Donald (1982), 'Aspects of the fifth generation: the Japanese knowledge bomb', in SPL International (1982).

Moto-Oka, Tohru (ed.) (1982), *Fifth Generation Computer Systems: Proceedings of the International Conference on Fifth Generation Computer Systems, Tokyo, Japan, October 19–22, 1981*, North Holland.

Scarrott, G. C. (ed.) (1983), *The Fifth Generation Computer Project: State of the Art Report*, Pergamon Infotech.

SPL International (1982), *The Fifth Generation – Dawn of the Second Computer Age*.

Yasukawa, H. (1983), 'LFG in Prolog: toward a formal system for representing grammatical relations', Icot Technical Report No. TR-019, 1983.

10

Applications of fifth generation computers

Discussions of potential applications of fifth generation computers must be in the context of the timescale of their development: the first full implementations of the new technology are scheduled for completion in the early 1990s. It is somewhat difficult to predict the requirements for computing facilities that far into the future. However, it is quite likely that intermediate results of fifth generation research will lead to new or enhanced computer applications before the main work is complete. It is also quite clear that the main thrust of the fifth generation programmes is capability driven — towards more intelligent computers — rather than demand driven, towards specific applications. Nevertheless, the fundamental concept of a fifth generation computer includes an intelligent user interface, making them potentially usable by a very large group of people, and the social aspects of the developments are regarded as very important.

With these reservations in mind, it is nevertheless possible to outline, with some measure of assurance, the likely application areas of fifth generation computers. Some are an extrapolation of present developments, such as expert systems, while others, such as voice-activated word processors, are entirely new. In essence, the primary role of a fifth generation computer is problem solving, its method of working is logical inference, and applications include areas of judgement (Sell, 1982). In this chapter, application areas are grouped by activity: industrial, military, commercial, design and educational applications, and expert systems. The intention is not to present an exhaustive list, nor to make any definite predictions of the future, but to discuss some of the potential applications of fifth generation computers, in order to provide concrete illustrations of the end products whose elements have been described in previous chapters.

10.1 INDUSTRIAL APPLICATIONS

The present generation of industrial robots have brought about a revolution in manufacturing, particularly in the automobile industry. On the one hand, they have played a vital part in the survival of vehicle manufacturers, through their increased productivity; on the other hand they have put thousands of workers out of their jobs. These first generation robots are very limited in their performance: each can do only a small range of tasks, and each task has to be programmed as a fixed sequence of operations. Research into the next generation of robots predates the fifth generation initiative, but has been assimilated to some extent into it. The aim is to produce robots with greatly increased intelligence, as well as visual and tactile sensory capabilities.

A new generation robot will be able to undertake a wide variety of tasks, within an overall framework of aims and objectives with which it is supplied. It will have a self-learning capability, and a high-level communication interface with its 'minder'. For example, a robot of this nature, given the objectives of a particular task, might be able to determine its own sequence of steps in order to carry out the task, and to vary these steps according to external requirements. It might evolve one sequence in order to perform the task as quickly as possible, and another to use as little energy as possible. By continuously monitoring its own performance, it might refine the sequences in the light of previous experience.

Robots are often installed as part of integrated flexible manufacturing systems, where all aspects of the process are under centralised computer control. The use of intelligent robots, coupled with similar advances in the overall manufacturing control systems, is likely to be as big an advance in manufacturing techniques as the original introduction of robots. It is also likely to have similar effects on jobs in these areas.

10.2 MILITARY APPLICATIONS

Military applications are one of the largest areas of use for fifth generation computers. They fall broadly into two classes: systems which are primarily of an advisory nature, and those which are almost entirely automatic (Taylor, 1983). In the second category, weapons systems of all kinds are being supplied with increased on-board intelligence. The ground-hugging Cruise missile represents the state of the art of contemporary control systems. It has digitised maps of the terrain it is to follow, and the location of its target programmed into it. It then follows a preset course, adjusting its altitude according to its on-board maps, and information received from its ground-scanning radar. An intelligent Cruise missile would be able to vary its course according to conditions encountered en route, take evasive action against missile defence systems, and (possibly) choose alternative targets according to tactical decisions made during its flight. This last option, bearing in mind the nuclear nature of Cruise missile warheads, is likely to be matter of bitter controversy. Similar 'smart' guidance systems, on a larger or smaller scale, are certain to be fitted to torpedoes, anti-aircraft missiles, anti-ship missiles and intercontinental ballistic missiles.

The proposed strategic defence systems currently at feasibility study stage rely entirely on intelligent computer systems for their operation. They propose to use a combination of satellite-based and ground-based weapons, based on lasers and other high-energy beam sources, to destroy large numbers of incoming missiles in flight. Some of their requirements are thought to be beyond even the scope of fifth generation computers: how to deal, in real time, with a full-scale ICBM attack, where each incoming missile has multiple warheads, independently targeted, and releases a number of dummy warheads in flight. If such anti-ballistic missile systems do prove feasible, they will require computer systems which can make very large numbers of strategic, tactical and operational decisions very rapidly, as well as performing the enormous numbers of calculations needed to track incoming missiles and control the defensive measures.

Military command, control and communications systems are becoming increasingly computerised, and the availability of computers with enhanced intelligence will enable new generations of these systems to be produced. Many of these systems are likely to be voice-activated, following a tradition already established for submarine control and similar systems. The very first application of electronic computers — cracking the codes of enemy communications — will benefit greatly from computers which can cope with natural language. Interactive tactical and operational decision support systems will assist the work of commanding officers at various levels. Electronic warfare — where each side attempts to intercept and disrupt the command and communications systems of the other — will take on a new dimension as computers are introduced which can make intelligent decisions at electronic speeds. Aerial and submarine warfare are conducted to an increasing extent by these methods, and research activities are particularly directed towards advances in these fields.

10.3 COMMERCIAL APPLICATIONS

Although the concept of an electronic office is taking much longer to become a reality than was at first predicted, the move towards office automation is steady and irreversible. The current goal is integrated office computer and communications networks, where all aspects of the business of a company — production, stock control, sales, purchases, payroll and accounting — are handled by a linked set of electronic systems. It is likely that fifth generation computers will enable an additional layer to be constructed above integrated business databases of this sort. The operational information in the database will form the raw material of a business knowledge base. On this knowledge base will be built decision support systems for managers, and in-depth analysis facilities enabling strategic evaluations to be made of business information. These will be of assistance in resource allocation, scheduling, market analysis and corporate planning.

At a more mundane level, the voice-activated word processor is one of the most specific measures of achievement of the goals of the fifth generation computer development programmes. Word processing is one of the commonest contemporary computer applications, and the ability to dictate to a word processor will be of great benefit (in addition to being a tantalising market opportunity for companies which can develop viable systems). A related application is automatic language translation systems. Ideally these will be totally automated, but in practice they are likely to be interactive with a skilled operator who deals with the situations where the automatic system cannot cope. Combining the two systems will, for example, enable simultaneous transcripts of the proceedings of international meetings to be produced in all the languages of the participants. Business, engineering and scientific documents could be dictated in one language at one site, and be transcribed and transmitted to another site where they are automatically translated, with only minimal delay. Voice-activated word processors and automatic language translation systems are under development in Britain as Alvey demonstrator projects, and in Japan.

10.4 DESIGN APPLICATIONS

Computer-aided design is an application area with a long and somewhat chequered history. CAD systems are now beginning to fulfil their early promises, and are an essential aspect of motor vehicle, ship, aeroplane and spacecraft design, as well as being the only way of developing modern integrated circuits. Fifth generation CAD systems will take over more and more of the actual drafting process, whether it be of a car component or a chip, and interact with their operators at the level of design specifications. Given the overall parameters of the performance of a product, as well as some general guidelines and constraints, the new generation of CAD systems will work out the details for themselves, based on very large and complex design databases, and knowledge bases of design methodology. As discussed in section 5.9, CAD systems of this sort are essential for the design of fifth generation computers themselves, and a cyclic development path is envisaged, with advances in computing systems being used to assist in the design of the next iteration.

Similar advances are expected in design support systems for computer software (section 6.5). Although the goal of an Ipse is less ambitious than automatic design from specification, it is intended to play a vital part in the cost-effective generation of a code which is proved to be correct and in accordance with specifications. Together, CAD systems for hardware and Ipses for software are likely to form integrated fifth generation systems design facilities, usable for a very wide range of electronics-based products.

10.5 EDUCATIONAL APPLICATIONS

Computer-assisted learning is an application area where many of the original expectations have not been fulfilled. The interaction between teacher and student is much more subtle and complex than was realised by the designers of early CAL systems. The advent of computers with enhanced intelligence, operating on knowledge bases rather than information bases, may bring about major advances, though it is unlikely that the central role of a teacher will be usurped by a computer. What may be possible are systems such as basic skills tutors, with abilities to diagnose, analyse and help correct faults of the student. Some preliminary work is under way on the design principles of such systems, which are not based on the traditional branching questionnaires, but on goal-directed questions and rule-based evaluation and assessment. Work is also under way on systems which model the typical ways in which students make errors, and use these models to help correct these errors.

A less controversial development is the evolution of educational databases into knowledge bases, which are accessible in a large subset of a natural language. These should help to overcome the reluctance on the part of many educationalists to use computers and allow teachers and students access to comprehensive stores of highly structured information.

10.6 EXPERT SYSTEMS

The application area of fifth generation computers with the greatest potential is expert systems. Expert systems have been a significant aspect of artificial intelligence research for many years, and a small number of systems have been in operational use for some time (the earliest dates back to 1965). They are already starting to have a general impact, but the advent of fifth generation computers should provide the vehicle for their widespread availability.

As mentioned in section 2.8, expert systems are the product of the application of techniques of artifical intelligence to specific fields. An expert system is a computer system which has assimilated some of the expert knowledge of a person, such as a doctor, geologist, analytical chemist or stock market trader. Some expert systems are intended for use as interactive advisers by the experts in the same field, others are used by less highly qualified or specialist personnel. Given a problem in its specialist field, an expert system is expected to solve the problem, and provide an explanation to the user of its line of reasoning if required. Most operate in an interactive mode, allowing the user to supply information in a flexible way, and providing intermediate conclusions as soon as these can be drawn. In some applications, the expert knowledge is 'fixed' into the system when it is created; in others the system is capable of learning from its own experience (including its own mistakes). At present two types of expert systems are available: those with the expertise in a particular field 'built in', and expert system shells, which have the general knowledge processing facilities, but where the specific expertise must be supplied by a knowledge engineer in conjunction with an expert in conjunction with an expert in order to create an operational system.

All expert systems operate on a knowledge base, which is generally updated as each new case is dealt with. Most have sets of rules expressing the 'tricks of their trade'. They have control techniques for applying the rules to the knowledge base in order to solve the problems posed to them (section 2.3). The earliest expert systems were confined to domains in which the knowledge is well-structured, according to the following criteria: a small search space, a consistent knowledge base with no contradictions, and reliable and static data provided by the user during interactions with the expert system (Alty and Coombs, 1984). Later systems have been able to relax these constraints to an increasing extent, allowing expert systems to be constructed in fields of increasing complexity. Fifth generation computers should allow them to be relaxed almost entirely, making it possible to design an expert system for use in a field where the knowledge base is very large, the knowledge may be vague, incomplete and contradictory, and the state of a problem may change during its analysis by the expert system. Most problems in the medical field fall into this latter category, and a real-time surgeon's assistant for use during complex operations is an example of what might be achieved when fifth generation computers are able to host expert systems.

Some of the areas of expertise tackled by early expert systems include: the diagnosis and treatment of infectious diseases (Mycin, Stanford University), geological exploration (Prospector, SRI International/US Geological Survey), general internal medicine (Internist, Pittsburgh University), the determination of chemical structures using mass spectrometer data (Dendral, Stanford University, the first operational expert system), the configuration of minicomputer systems (R1, Digital Equipment Corporation) and the design of genetics experiments (Molgen, Stanford University). Medical expert systems are likely to remain a significant field for development — the goal of a diagnostic aid for general practitioners is being actively pursued at a number of centres. One of the Alvey demonstrator projects is an expert system for use when claiming social security benefits, the UK social security system being almost impossible to comprehend without an expert of some sort. Other possibilities for expert systems include various aspects of the law, the design of road and rail networks, taxation, commercial market analysis, weather forecasting, financial management and a large number of strategic and tactical military systems.

10.7 CONCLUSION

The point must be stressed that at this stage it is not possible to predict specific applications of fifth generation computers with any certainty. The general application areas are clear, as is the intended group of potential users, from the conceptual definition of a fifth generation computer. The nature and timing of specific applications depends on the order in which some of the fundamental problems of fifth generation research are solved: voice recognition, image processing and, above all, knowledge representation in the general sense. It is likely that a cyclic sequence of development will ensue towards the end of the fifth generation research programmes, with products becoming available as various aspects of the research are complete, and these products being used in the development of subsequent stages. Whether a commercial return is ever attained for all the investment in fifth generation research and development remains to be seen.

REFERENCES

Alty, J. L., and Coombs, M. J. (1984), *Expert Systems: Concepts and Examples*, National Computing Centre.

Sell, P. S. (1982), 'New computer applications: user and social acceptability of the fifth generation proposals', in SPL International (1982).

SPL International (1982), *The Fifth Generation – Dawn of the Second Computer Age*.

SPL International (1983), *Fifth Generation World Conference, 1983.*

Taylor, John (1983), 'Knowledge-based systems in defence: applications and implications', in SPL International (1983).

11

The fifth generation in perspective

The extent to which the central goals of the fifth generation research programmes will be attained is by no means certain at this stage, and a number of the consequences of the initiative depend on which targets are met by which development teams in which countries, and how these developments are exploited. The bulk of this chapter assumes that these goals are attained, at least to an extent where intelligent knowledge-based systems are a practical proposition; the question of the likely success of the whole scheme is left to the final section.

Fifth generation computer systems are one element in the broader field of information technology, which also encompasses electronic control systems and telecommunications. Information technology is an agent of change, very powerful in itself, but only one of a number of technological pressure points. Others include advances in biochemistry and genetic engineering, and further uses, both peaceful and otherwise, of nuclear energy. Technological change is in turn one element in a larger matrix of pressures for change. Other forces include religious, political and economic pressure, the pressure of expanding populations and diminishing resources, and the environmental pressures as our small planet becomes increasingly choked with pollutants. At frequent intervals these pressures erupt into wars, terrorist attacks, famines, strikes, protests or the extinction of yet another species of plant or animal, which no intelligent computer or miracle of genetic engineering can retrieve. Information technology operates in the same arena as all the other forces for change, it interacts with them, and its consequences are as complex and difficult to understand as those of the resurgence of fundamentalist Islam.

It is against this background that the consequences of the development of intelligent computer systems must be evaluated. The consequences will be felt by individuals, corporations and nations in a number of ways, and could be very far-reaching.

11.1 THE IMPACT OF INTELLIGENT KNOWLEDGE-BASED SYSTEMS

From the very outset, the central role of information processing systems in all walks of life has been a major driving force behind the development of the new generation of computers. This is particularly the case in Japan: 'Information processing systems will be central tools in all areas of social activity to include economics, industry, art and science, administration, international relations, education, culture and daily life and so forth' (JIPDEC, 1981). Intelligent computer systems will have a major, and sometimes dramatic, impact in all these spheres. A few possibilities are quoted below by way of example.

The medical field is probably the most useful body of knowledge and expertise in existence at present. It has all the hallmarks of the fifth generation: a very large corpus, based on a mixture of firmly established scientific principles, working hypotheses, rules of thumb, and accumulated experience with as yet no formal validation. It also has very large gaps, and contains areas which are vague and sometimes contradictory. Nevertheless the majority of people alive today owe their health or even their lives to modern medicine and its practitioners. If fifth generation computers are able to assimilate substantial portions of contemporary medical knowledge, and provide expert systems which enhance and amplify the skills of medical practitioners, the benefits on a worldwide scale will be enormous. Many Third World countries have endemic shortages of doctors, and base their rural health services on paramedical staff, along the lines of the Chinese 'barefoot doctors'. If these paramedical staff could be provided with small diagnostic aids, robustly constructed for their working environments, and voice-driven, the quality of their first-line services could improve greatly. This in turn would bring about a big improvement in the health services of these countries.

The management of natural resources, both renewable, such as timber, and finite, such as oil, is an issue of increasing significance. The situation is very complex, with geological, ecological, economic and political factors to take into consideration. The use of expert systems and decision support systems in the evolution of management policies and the implementation of these policies could bring great benefits. One of the most difficult problems which will face Britain in the first decades of the new century falls precisely into this category: how to manage the depletion and possibly the exhaustion of the North Sea oil reserves.

There are a number of areas of social administration, in particular taxation, social security benefit schemes, housing and transport policies, where the situation has become so complex that it verges on the unmanageable. The use of intelligent computer systems, using knowledge inferred from the databases which are already coming into existence in these areas, could help to restore some degree of comprehensibility to the situation, and help to eliminate many of the errors, injustices and delays which have been passively accepted as part of these bureaucracies for decades. There are always the dangers, when using computers for social administration, of infringements of individual liberties: the fifth generation, with its potential for intelligent decision-making on social or personal data, may give rise to concerns over and above those created by the introduction of conventional computers.

In the business world, it is already conventional wisdom that the profitability of an organisation is directly proportional to the quality of its information systems. This will no doubt continue to be true as intelligent decision support systems and corporate knowledge bases become available. Many firms, large and small, will stand or fall according to the way in which they manage the transition to the new generation technology. The rewards of success will be great: a much higher standard of management and planning, and optimised production, marketing, distribution, credit control and other business procedures. However, in the economic climate of the next decade, which is likely to be at least as harsh as that at present, firms that cannot compete at the national and international levels which will become the norm, will not survive.

The employment consequences of fifth generation computers are likely to be as complex as those of contemporary information technology: the direct creation and support of some jobs in the IT industry, the indirect creation and support of a large number of jobs through the contribution to higher productivity, and the loss of many jobs where the work is taken over by computer or computer-controlled processes. As discussed above, the companies which thrive, and thus provide secure employment for their workers, will be those with effective information systems. The difference will be that the threshold for substitution of people by electronic systems will be higher − well into the lower and middle strata of management. Companies will be able to operate with fewer managers, possibly in new management structures, all working with management support systems linked to the corporate knowledge base.

It is quite likely that the advent of fifth generation computers coincides with, and is an integral part of, a general improvement in the standards and quality of work in all spheres. Consumers are coming to expect better design, higher quality, increased safety standards and lower energy consumption from goods of all types, and faster, friendlier and more efficient services from the private and the public sector. The widespread use of computers with enhanced intelligence will greatly assist in this process, which may have far-reaching social and economic consequences.

11.2 MILITARY IMPLICATIONS

The consequences of the widespread military application of new generation computers are serious, and are already becoming the topic of debate. The new technology will continue the trend towards the increased mechanisation of warfare, and for the first time transfer some tactical and even strategic military decision-making to computer-assisted systems, or even fully automated systems. For example, the majority of the operational decisions taken by a strategic defence system will have to be taken automatically, in view of the speed at which the system must respond. This raises three problems: the ethics of delegating military decision-making to computers, the danger of a conflict being started inadvertently by a computer malfunction, and the possibility of a devastating military defeat through the malfunction or failure of a critical electronic system. The latter points worry a large number of the IT professionals working in these fields, who are not convinced that all the errors latent in a system of the complexity of those envisaged can ever be detected and corrected.

11.3 THE IT MARKETPLACE

The information technology marketplace has never been a refuge for the fainthearted, and seems to alternate between periods of solid optimism and gloom and confusion. The semiconductor market has a cyclic pattern of worldwide shortage and over-supply, with prices fluctuating accordingly. Many investors are reluctant to risk their capital in a field which, although growing very rapidly, is subject to so many upheavals. In a field of such rapid innovation, and consequent obsolescence, most products are fortunate if they have a five-year market lifetime. With high development costs for hardware and software products, the difference between large profits and large losses often hinges on a small number of sales.

The fifth generation looks set to raise the stakes even higher. There will be a shift from labour-intensive development of hardware and software to capital-intensive techniques based on silicon foundries and integrated software development environments. The very complex nature of fifth generation systems means that even with state-of-the-art development aids, the costs of bringing a new product to the marketplace will be very high. However, if intelligent user interfaces live up to their promises, the market for fifth generation products will be much larger, extending, with suitable development aid, deeply into the Third World. Conventional computer systems will rapidly become obsolete, as they are replaced by equivalent systems with enhanced intelligence. Similarly, there is a danger that IT professionals with conventional skills will suffer the same fate, as they are replaced by knowledge engineers using fifth generation systems design tools.

As has been the case with the previous four generations of computers, the fifth generation programme is primarily a capability-driven endeavour. The Japanese initiative, which started the worldwide effort, was inspired by general social and economic considerations, but not by precisely identified market needs. The point has occasionally been made that computers are a solution looking for a problem, and the fifth generation is not automatically an exception to this. The effort of translating the theoretical advances in knowledge processing and voice recognition into practical, marketable and profitable products is at least as challenging as the development of intelligent computers in the first place. Assuming that the theoretical advances are made, it is this final hurdle which will ultimately determine whether all the time, effort and money invested in the fifth generation programmes pays off.

11.4 THE IT NATIONAL LEAGUE

Information technology is, in spite of the problems mentioned in the previous section, becoming a significant industrial sector. It is a source of economic growth and stability, a major employer, a generator of wealth and, with its permanent commitment to research and development, a reasonable guarantee of future economic viability for the host country. It is also becoming the key to the economic viability of the industrial, commercial and financial sectors, as they come to depend on electronic systems for all aspects of their operations. Accordingly, the strength and size of the IT industrial sector in every developed nation is a matter of critical economic and political importance. There have been many changes of place in the world IT league since the early days when the USA was the leading hardware supplier and the UK the world leader in software. The situation is further complicated by the transnational nature of most of the leading IT corporations, and the fact that most computers are an aggregation of components made all over the world. Some chips are even flown halfway around the world between wafer fabrication and packaging stages.

The fifth generation is almost certain to cause yet another shuffling of the pack, depending on how well, and how quickly, the various IT groupings exploit the advances of the new technology. Most of the national development programmes have restrictions on the transfer of the research findings to companies within the host country or region, but the effectiveness of this policy remains to be tested. As always, the Eastern Bloc countries lag behind their Western counterparts, but are endeavouring to keep up by every means at their disposal.

The point cannot be over-emphasised that, for the first time in history, Japan has made the running: the name, concept and development path of fifth generation computers are all due to the Japanese initiative. Although there is at present no obvious ranking in the progress made by the development teams, the undoubted depth of commitment to the Japanese project, together with Japan's proven record as an implementer and perfecter of established technology, may be decisive. The USA, with its depth of experience in artificial intelligence, and its sound IT establishment, is in a very strong position. It is significant that IBM has not made any public commitment to the fifth generation. IBM has traditionally left others to innovate, and then entered the market when the first round of dust has settled. It has done so with overwhelming effect in mainframe computers in the 1950s and microcomputers in the 1980s, and could well repeat this performance in intelligent systems in the 1990s. In Britain and Europe, the situation is much more in balance. Britain's fortunes have gradually declined during the early 1980s from being a significant computer hardware and software exporter to being a net importer. Although the UK has a tradition of innovation in computing, the track record for development and exploitation is not as healthy, and artificial intelligence research in Britain nearly came to a complete standstill during the 1970s. In Europe as a whole, the question is whether the national producers and consumers can be persuaded to form a sufficiently coherent market to compete as a unit against the Americans and the Japanese.

11.5 HUMAN AND ARTIFICIAL INTELLIGENCE

When commenting on the consequences of the advent of intelligent computer systems, the dangers of indulging in flights of science-fiction fancy must be avoided. Although they will be much more intelligent in certain respects than contemporary computers, fifth generation computers will come nowhere near to rivalling human intelligence in general terms. Fifth generation computers will not be able to pass the Turing test; it is unlikely that they will be of use as a vehicle for the ultimate challenge of artificial intelligence – the automation of human common sense.

Fifth generation computers are not usurping human mental powers; they are complementing them, albeit at a higher level than before. The interaction between a computer and its user will move to a higher conceptual level – in many cases a rich subset of natural language – but the user will be in no doubt that he or she is using a computer and not interacting with a person. A fair amount of intelligence and knowledge is passing to the electronic side of the user interface, but in-depth analysis, understanding, inspiration, creativity and initiative are still firmly in the domain of the user. In order to make the best use of intelligent computer systems, a fair amount of intelligence will be required of the user.

One can perceive, in the spirit of Teilhard de Chardin, a continuum of intelligence ranging from simple sensory responses, through the manipulation of data, human intelligence, knowledge and wisdom, into the realms of religion and mysticism. Computers have travelled some distance along this road, past the milestones of calculating, sorting, selection and making complex combinations of binary decisions. They are at present entering the region of expertise in particular fields, as they draw inferences from knowledge bases to offer reasoned advice. But the distance travelled is tiny compared with what lies ahead, and the route is not marked. Nor is it clear that computers as we understand them today, or as they are evolving towards a new iteration, are the right vehicles to be travelling much further along this path. The present state of affairs is aptly summarised in the words of IT journalist Rex Malik: a computer is 'an amplifier of active intelligence'. This situation is likely to remain the case for some time in the future, beyond the timescale of the fifth generation.

11.6 CONCLUSION

The central question is whether the goals of the fifth generation computer programmes will be attained. This question must remain open for the time being, but the consensus view is that the direction of research is right — 'the path to the Fifth Generation Systems must contain many risks, and some failures, but there is no other way' (Feigenbaum, 1982). It is significant that all the early checkpoints of the Japanese programme have been reached on or ahead of schedule, and there have been no defections amongst any of the participants. Recruitment of knowledge engineers and personnel with artificial intelligence training or experience is rapidly increasing throughout the IT world, and a number of hardware and software products with expert system or artificial intelligence capabilities are beginning to appear on the market. The fifth generation initiative has given the IT community worldwide a sense of direction and purpose — 'at the very least, Japan has set the world computing targets for the rest of the decade and beyond' (Bob Muller, SPL International).

A number of specific hurdles can be identified, over which the fifth generation development teams must pass. The most challenging is undoubtedly knowledge representation in the general sense. If a firm foundation for knowledge representation techniques is established, then a number of associated obstacles will be much easier to scale. These include natural language interpretation and voice recognition. On the systems design side, the main obstacle is a coherent overall architecture for parallel processing systems. Associated with it is the right programming language (or set of programming languages) to work efficiently on parallel architectures and at the same time satisfy the logical requirements of intelligent knowledge-based systems. Possibly the easiest hurdle of all is the requirement for an improvement of at least two orders of magnitude in the number of elements on a chip, and the processing speeds which can be achieved. The last hurdle in the race is the applications hurdle — to bring the capabilities of intelligent computing systems into focus on the demands for productive, beneficial and cost-effective information technology systems of the 1990s.

Although there is a single, well-defined goal of a complete fifth generation computer at the end of the road, the separate paths which converge towards it are all viable research efforts in their own right. The most cautious scenario is the Alvey approach, of enabling technologies which lead to intelligent systems, but which, by accident or design, have a great many incidental benefits. Research into VLSI, new computer architectures and software engineering is of great benefit to conventional computing systems, and to all the other branches of information technology. Work on knowledge bases feeds back to databases. Every incremental improvement in user interfaces is beneficial to computer systems of all types.

Ultimately the success or failure of the fifth generation initiative depends on the number of IT practitioners who have some knowledge and understanding of the project and its implications, and will be on hand to put the developments to work as soon as they become available. It is to this group that this book is dedicated, with the aim of keeping information technology on course to becoming the world's largest industrial sector by the turn of the century.

REFERENCES

Feigenbaum, Edward (1982), 'Innovation and symbol manipulation in fifth generation computers', in Moto-Oka (1982), pp. 223—226.

JIPDEC (1981), 'Preliminary report on study and research on fifth-generation computers', Japan Information Processing Development Centre, in Moto-Oka (1982), pp. 3—89.

Moto-Oka, Tohru (ed.) (1982), *Fifth Generation Computer Systems: Proceedings of the International Conference on Fifth Generation Computer Systems, Tokyo, Japan, October 19—22, 1981*, North Holland.

Glossary of terms

abstract data type
a class of computer data defined in terms of its logical properties, independent of its physical representation in the computer system.

algorithm
a description of the steps of a particular hardware or software task.

allophone
an elementary sound component of speech.

Alvey programme
the UK fifth generation computer development programme.

application programming language
a programming language in which programs are structured as functions operating on abstract data types, and there are no destructive assignments.

artificial intelligence
the ability of a computer to behave in a way which, if it were the behaviour of a person, would be regarded as intelligent.

combinatorial explosion	the situation which arises when the number of steps required to carry out an operation such as searching exceeds by many orders of magnitude the capacity of the computer to process in an acceptable time.
communicating sequential processes	a set of tasks, each carried out by a sequential processing element in a computer, which can transfer information between each other at specified stages.
computer	a machine which, under the control of a stored program, automatically inputs, processes and outputs data and which may also store, retrieve, transmit and receive data.
computer-aided design (CAD)	the use of computerised equipment for design and drafting tasks.
computer-assisted learning (CAL)	the use of computers to assist in teaching and training.
data independence	the separation of the logical data model of a database from the physical structure of the stored data.
dataflow architecture	the arrangement of the parallel processing elements in a computer in a network so that data flows from one element to another during the execution of a program.
decision support system	a computer system used by managers which operates on the knowledge base of the particular organisation and gives reasoned advice to assist in making management decisions.
declarative programming language	a programming language which allows tasks to be described in terms of the data structures to be used, and what processing operations are to be carried out on the data, rather than how the processing is to be done, as in the case of procedural languages.

declarativist knowledge representation	the representation of knowledge independently of the control procedures which are to be used when processing the knowledge.
Defense Advanced Research Project Agency (Darpa)	the branch of the US Department of Defense responsible for fifth generation projects.
direct memory access (DMA)	direct access by peripheral devices to the main store of a processor, bypassing the processing registers.
enabling technology	one of the four technologies — VLSI, intelligent knowledge-based systems, software engineering and intelligent user interfaces — which paves the way for fifth generation computer systems.
Entscheidungsproblem	the problem of whether there exists a definite method which, when applied to any mathematical problem, will decide whether or not it has a solution.
Esprit	the EEC fifth generation computer development programme.
evidential reasoning	the analysis of evidence such as that presented in a criminal trial in order to reach a consensus view and draw general conclusions.
expert system	a computer system which automates a measure of human expertise in a particular field.
expert system shell	an empty expert system structure, into which a particular field of expertise is built.
fifth generation computer	a computer which uses inference to draw reasoned conclusions from a knowledge base, and interacts with its users via an intelligent user interface.
first generation computer	a computer using valves as its basic technology.
fourth generation computer	a computer using microprocessors and LSI chips as its basic technology.

fractal	a type of mathematical function consisting of a sequence of discontinuous line or area segments which are recursively contained within each line or area.
frame	a structure for storing one node in a knowledge representation network.
functional decomposition	the specification of the structure of a program by starting with a top-level function, and decomposing this function into sets of functions at lower levels which together implement the definition of the higher level functions.
gigabyte	one thousand million bytes.
graph reduction architecture	the arrangement of the parallel processing elements in a computer so that they execute the graph structure of a program directly.
hardware	the physical components of a computer system.
heuristic	by methods of common sense or rules of thumb.
Horn clause	a type of clause in predicate logic which has one or more conditions linked by the AND operator, and a single conclusion.
icon	a visual symbol which appears on the display screen of a computer as part of its user interface.
image processing	the processing of visual images such as those from a video camera by computer.
inference processor	the element of a fifth generation computer system which draws reasoned conclusions from knowledge.
information systems factory	an integrated hardware and software computer design and development facility.

Institute for New Generation Computer Technology (Icot)	the centre of the Japanese fifth generation computer development programme.
integrated programming support environment (Ipse)	a compatible set of tools based on a methodology for all the phases of software development and operation, supporting both technical and management activities.
intelligent knowledge-based system (IKBS)	a computer system which uses inference to apply knowledge to perform a task.
intelligent user interface	the user interface of a computer which matches the way of thinking and methods of communication of a user in approaching the task.
knowledge base	the body of knowledge stored in a fifth generation computer system from which inferences are drawn.
knowledge engineer	a person who designs expert systems or intelligent knowledge-based systems.
lambda calculus	a methodology based on a formal notation for the expression of mathematical or logical statements.
logical inference per second (lips)	the measure of the speed of performance of a fifth generation computer system.
mathematical induction	a technique of proving certain types of mathematical theorems by showing that, if the theorem is true in a particular case, then it is also true in the 'next' case.
megabyte	one million bytes.
Microelectronic and Computer Technology Corporation (MCC)	a company sponsored by a consortium of USA IT corporations which undertakes fifth generation research and development projects on behalf of its sponsors.
micron	one millionth of a metre.

minimax	a game-playing strategy which minimises the maximum possible advantage to an opponent of any particular move in the game.
Ministry of International Trade and Industry (MITI)	the branch of the Japanese Civil Service responsible for industrial development.
module	a system with a precisely defined boundary and standardised external interfaces.
mouse	a hand-held object which, when moved over a flat surface, causes a pointer on a computer display screen to move in a corresponding way.
nanosecond	one thousand millionth of a second.
non-procedural programming language	a class of programming languages including declarative and applicative languages which specify what processing operations are required without specifying how the processing steps are to be carried out.
parallel control flow	the delegation of control in a parallel computer system from a central point to two or more parallel sequential processes.
parallel processing	the execution of more than one sequence of processing steps simultaneously within a computer system.
parsing	the determination of the syntactic structure of a program or text in a natural language.
personal sequential inference processor (PSI)	the Prolog-based workstations used by the staff at the Icot centre.
pipeline	a set of dedicated processing elements connected together in a sequence, each carrying out one step of the particular operation.
predicate	a logical relationship.

predicate calculus the formal techniques for applying the rules of inference to predicates.

proceduralist knowledge representation a technique for knowledge representation where the control structures for processing the knowledge are an integral part of the knowledge itself.

procedural programming language a programming language which requires that the detailed steps of the processing of data be specified for each task.

processing array a vector or matrix of identical processing elements all working synchronously.

production system a set of statements describing the logical properties of a knowledge base.

program a set of instructions to control the operation of a computer.

regular parallelism parallel processing carried out by identical processing elements operating synchronously.

relational database a database structured as sets of instances of relations between individual data items.

rendezvous a point of communication between two sequential processes.

rule of inference a general rule which is used in predicate calculus.

script a description of the context within which communication in a natural language takes place between a computer and a user.

search space the set of states to be generated and tested or examined during a search.

second generation computer a computer using discrete transistors as its basic technology.

semantic gap the gap between the low-level hardware capabilities of a computer and the high-level application-oriented demands placed on it by its software.

semantic network	a technique of knowledge represent-ation by means of nodes representing objects and arcs representing relations between them.
semantics	the meaning behind a passage in a natural language.
silicon foundry	an integrated set of computer-aided design and fabrication facilities for VLSI chips.
software	the programs which control the operation of a computer.
software engineering	the profession dedicated to the design, development and maintenance of computer software in a managed way, subject to strict cost, time and performance constraints.
software evolution	a holistic view of the cycle of stages in the life of a software object: design, development, commissioning, main-tenance and revision.
speech synthesis	the generation of vocal sounds by a computer from internally stored text.
state machine approach	a technique of software design by representing the task to be performed as a finite state machine.
state space	the set of states to be generated and tested or examined during a search.
stepwise refinement	a technique of software design which starts with a top-level description of the task to be performed and proceeds by expanding the stages in progres-sively more detail.
syntax	the structure of a natural language or a programming language, as determined by a set of formal rules.
system	a set of inter-related elements, enclosed by a well-defined boundary, which together achieve, or attempt to achieve, specific aims and objectives.

systolic array	an assembly of special-purpose processing elements on a single chip which are designed to carry out certain specific processing algorithms.
third generation computer	a computer having integrated circuits (but not microprocessors) as its basic technology.
transputer	a single-chip processor, with an on-board memory, designed for very high throughput of data, in order to form part of a parallel processor architecture.
Turing machine	a theoretical computing machine, designed by Alan Turing, which can, in principle, solve any problem which can be expressed in the form of an algorithm.
user interface	the point of contact between a computer system and the person using it.
very large scale integration (VLSI)	the inclusion of very large numbers (tens of thousands or more) of discrete elements on a single integrated circuit.
voice recognition	the ability of a computer system to recognise and interpret spoken input.
wafer-scale integration	the fabrication of a single 5 cm square chip, with a very large number of discrete elements, on a silicon wafer.
window	a portion of the display screen of a computer which displays the output from one program, while another program is running and being displayed on the rest of the screen.

Index

DIS